EDUMATCH SNAPSHOT IN EDUCATION 2020

REMOTE LEARNING EDITION

BREANN FENNELL TISHA PONCIO
WINIFRED WINSTON KRISTEN KOPPERS
JAMI FOWLER-WHITE BRUCE REICHER
MARIE MCCUMBER ALEXES TERRY
MELODY MCALLISTER ILENE WINOKUR
DEBORAH KERBY AUBREY JONES
JERRY TOUPS, JR. JASON ALLEN
MATTHEW RHOADS DAWN BERKELEY
ALICE ASPINALL LISA NOWAKOWSKI
MELISSA TORRENCE STEPHANIE JACOBS
MELINDA VANDEVORT REBECCA GIBBONEY
ERIN KIGER JESSICA REED REGINA MOORE
LYNN THOMAS MARVIA DAVIDSON

Edited by
SARAH THOMAS

Copyright © 2020
Published by EduMatch®
PO Box 150324, Alexandria, VA 22315
www.edumatchpublishing.com

All rights reserved. No portion of this book may be reproduced in any form without permission from the publisher, except as permitted by U.S. copyright law. For permissions contact sarah@edumatch.org.

ISBN: 978-1-953852-05-2

CONTENTS

1. SUDDENLY SUPERSTITIOUS   1
   BreAnn Fennell
2. I DIDN'T SIGN UP FOR THIS   5
   Tisha Poncio
3. SPECIAL EDUCATION IN THE AGE OF COVID-19:   13
   HOW TO WIN OVER DYSLEXIA
   Winifred A. Winston (@soallcanread)
4. LEARNING HOW TO TEACH REMOTELY   25
   Kristen Koppers, NBCT
5. REFLECTION TIP #12   31
   What practices are you integrating into your Blended Learning Classroom?
   Jami Fowler-White, NBCT
6. REMOTE PD IS LIKE A 24 HOUR EDCAMP   49
   Bruce Reicher
7. LET'S LEARN OUTSIDE   53
   Marie K. McCumber
8. THE POWER OF REPRESENTATION   57
   Alexes M. Terry
9. THE WORK IN BECOMING AN ANTI-RACIST EDUCATOR   63
   Melody McAllister
10. BELONGING BEFORE BLOOM, NOT MASLOW BEFORE BLOOM   71
    Dr. Ilene Winokur
11. TALKING ABOUT SUICIDE WITH CHILDREN   89
    Dr. Deborah Kerby, Ed. D.
12. THERE ARE NO BAD KIDS   95
    Aubrey Jones
13. NON-VERBALLY COMMUNICATING LOVE   99
    Jerry Toups, Jr.

14. TO BE YOUNG, GIFTED, TALENTED, AND BLACK — 115
The Struggles of Black Boys in American Public Schools' Special Education Programs
Jason B. Allen

15. NAVIGATING FALL 2020 AND BEYOND — 123
An Organizational Framework to Navigate Between Online, Blended, and Traditional Educational Settings
Matthew C. Rhoads, Ed.D.

16. SIX PRINCIPLES FOR A ROBUST TECHNOLOGY INTEGRATION PLAN — 133
Dawn Carrera Berkeley

17. POSITIVE MATH TALK — 139
Alice Aspinall

18. MATHREPS — 149
Lisa M. Nowakowski

19. 2020 VISION OF DIGITAL CITIZENSHIP — 159
Melissa Torrence

20. COACHING WITH CLASS — 173
Stephanie D. Jacobs

21. EDUCATIONAL BLACKSMITHING — 189
Melinda Vandevort

22. A SPIN ON SERIOUS — 197
Rebecca Gibboney

23. JUGGLE THE STRUGGLE — 207
The Choice to Serve
Erin B. Kiger

24. BECOMING THE TEACHER I WAS MEANT TO BE — 211
Jessica Reed, Ed.S.

25. OVERCOMING BARRIERS & FINDING MY PASSION — 217
Regina A. Moore, M.Ed

26. YOU AND OTHER YS — 223
Lynn Thomas

27. TAKE TIME TO REST — 229
Marvia Davidson

Acknowledgments — 237
EduMatch Books Released in 2020 — 239

1

SUDDENLY SUPERSTITIOUS

BREANN FENNELL

Frightened by Friday the 13th, I was suddenly superstitious.

Friday the thirteenth was just any other day,
That was until Covid came our way.
The teachers were full of fear and worry,
We changed our lesson plans in quite a hurry.
I was suddenly superstitious.

Black Cats weren't crossing my path,
But I found myself creating videos about Math.
Fear of the unknown was in our hearts,
We all sought comfort in the arts.
I was suddenly superstitious.

Google conferencing became the new norm,
No one taught us this online form.
Parents and teachers were working from home,
Calling our loved ones on the phone.
No longer... superstitious.

Through all the newscasts and fear,
I became a teacher of the year.
Representing the mighty profession,
Wanting to learn and make a connection.
I can't be superstitious.

We can keep waiting for twenty-twenty-one,
Nothing will change if you just make fun.
Worried about how we are treating each other,
Wanting to protect our grandpa and mother.
It's more than superstitions.

Delivering meals to the homes of children,
Sharing great books that are one in a million.
Teachers are trying their best,
We keep signing on; we don't rest.
I'm not superstitious; I have hope.

BreAnn Fennell

BreAnn Fennell is a 1st and 2nd grade looping teacher at Reagan Elementary in Ashland City School District. She has earned the title of Ohio Teacher of the Year for 2021 for District 5. She has 10 years of teaching experience, educating students in 1st, 2nd, and 3rd grades. She also taught Preschool while attending college. She believes that early education and interventions can change the course of a child's life.

Fennell holds a bachelor's degree in early childhood education with an endorsement in reading from Ashland University and a 4-5 generalist endorsement from The Ohio State University. She has a master's degree in Curriculum and Instruction from Ashland University. She is always learning and serving the world of education through trainings, presentations, and committees. She desires to return to school for her PHD.

Fennell is the author of children's books including *Play? Yay!*, *Choose Your Cheer*, and *Play? Yay! Baby Talk*. She is a defender of play in the classroom and looks for ways to incorporate fun into learning. She believes in the power of play for social, emotional, and motor skills and has volunteered her time to have a Lego Club for kindergarten through third grade students. She is the founder of the Young Author's Workshop at Ashland City Schools. She loves books and is always looking for ways to integrate reading into the classroom and promote literacy in the community.

2

I DIDN'T SIGN UP FOR THIS

TISHA PONCIO

The thing I know for sure about teachers is at their very core, they are meant to serve, and they will do whatever is possible to get the job done, empower their students, and continue teaching.

Teachers, by their very nature, are accustomed to "expect the unexpected" because they all know that any plan is subject to change. They are used to dealing with last-minute schedule changes in their day, having to change lesson plans dependent on technology that may not be available, or put on a brave face and tackle all of the expectations for a new school year. However, in the spring of 2020, teachers across the globe were faced with an almost impossible situation: school closings, requirements for remote learning, and countless students and parents thrown into a forced remote learning environment. Some educators even juggled remote teaching of hundreds of students while supporting and caring for their children at the same time. The difficulty was that every teacher, parent, and student cried, "I didn't sign up for this!" Many teachers were not prepared to take their in-person classroom to a virtual setting overnight (which they did), and the majority of schools were not equipped to make such a fast transition to offering tech equipment, tech support, new digital support tools, or implementation of new learning management systems.

What I Know For Sure

The thing I know for sure about teachers is at their very core, they are meant to serve, and they will do whatever is possible to get the job done, empower their students, and continue teaching. With all of the minute-by-minute changes and requirements they faced, teachers were unsure of the future of their classrooms. Spring of 2020 morphed into "emergency online teaching," and educators did the best they could with what they had to keep the learning experiences going. As the fall semester approached, multiple high-risk educators or those that cared for high-risk family members were fearful of going back into the classroom. They were unsure of just how protected they would be from Covid19 and had difficulty wrapping their minds around mask management, cleaning and disinfecting classrooms, protecting themselves, and still meeting and teaching their learning goals and objectives. Numerous educators updated wills and worried about their well-being and the safety of their families.

Some educators did not feel supported by their school, state, or national leaders. While this is disappointing for various reasons, educators globally found support from each other on social media platforms. Twitter has been a source of comfort and comradeship for educators for a while, but educators have also taken to TikTok, Facebook Groups, and Instagram to grow their PLN (personal learning network), share resources, find creative ideas, and encouragement. More than ever, teachers now have access to a multitude of free webinars, free virtual conferences, and availability to recordings even if they missed the live sessions.

As summer faded and schools across the globe began making decisions on whether to open with face-to-face instruction, continue with only remote learning or roll out a hybrid learning plan with teachers fulfilling face-to-face instruction and online instruction at the same time, educators' anxieties became increasingly apparent. Expectations and procedures seemed inconsistent, and K-12 educators felt the need to scramble and cram knowledge of new digital tools and new blended or virtual learning strategies. I found that teachers needed more support than I ever predicted with blended learning/remote learning tips as they started planning for the upcoming school year. Here are tips I have consistently shared with teachers:

Best Practices While Using Technology to Save Time

1. Be Flexible (Romero & Barberà, 2011)
2. Model Digital Citizenship (Huang, 2002)
3. Move from Teacher to Facilitator (Huang, 2002)
4. Set & Communicate Clear Expectations/Goals (Herrington, Reeves, Oliver, & Woo 2004)
5. Create a Culture of Learning, Fun, Voice & Choice (McCombs 2015)
6. Follow Age + Screen Time Recommendations (Noonoo, 2020)
7. Move from Completion to Creation (Elliot, 2007)
8. Offer Immediate Feedback and Time for Reflection (Huang, 2002)
9. Reassess Assessments (An, 2012; Rubenstein, 2010)

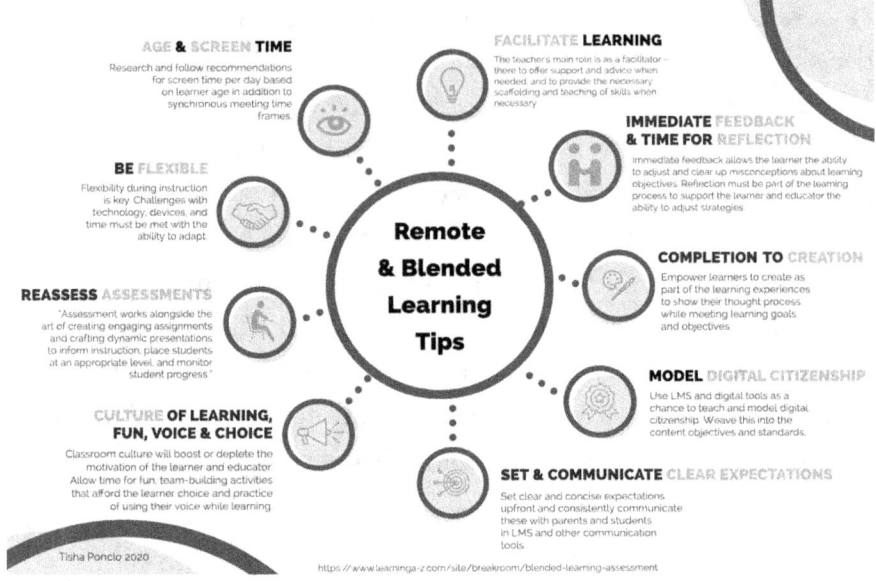

For the majority of educators, the pressure of teaching in 2020 was insurmountable. More than ever, educators needed to band together and share resources, knowledge, and tips. To create spaces of support, several educational technology companies provided free professional development webinars and used their platforms to not only share how to use their tools in a virtual setting, but also to discuss issues that directly affected educators like social-emotional learning, race and culture, remote and blended learning strategies, and overall lessons or takeaways from the spring of 2020. I was overwhelmed by the number of attendees signing up for the webinars in which I was involved and felt that the numbers were a definite outcry for learning and support and a reflection of how things were going for so many educators around the world. One Wakelet webinar offering I did along with Wakelet's Misbah Gedal in August of 2020 focused on remote learning. There were 2400 signups for the webinar, and over 1300 teachers joined in for the live session. Many companies that offered free webinars had such an increase in attendee overflow they had to offer their webinars via YouTube Live or Facebook Live in addition to their typical platforms to ensure accessibility to all. This was very telling: teachers wanted and needed to learn, to come together, and to share ideas more than ever before. Learning and brainstorming ideas on how to engage students, collaborate with content, and be better than before eased the anxieties many were experiencing.

Moving Forward

As educators, we must forever embrace the idea of continuous learning. With a total of twenty years in education, I know how easy it is to fall into the familiar and claim "this is the way I have always done it," but I also know that some of my best years have occurred when I let go, tried a new idea or allowed room for others to suggest ideas I would have never thought of alone. No, we may not have signed up to teach from home virtually or even teach face-to-face simultaneously with virtual students, and many of us did not get degrees in online learning or blended learning. However, the very nature of our being reminds us that teaching and learning are naturally what we do, and that does not stop when the academic calendar stops or even for a pandemic. Extended learning of our craft should be a prerequisite each year, but especially for 2020. We cannot depend on someone else to require the training or mandate our completion of learning modules for best practices and technology integration. We must surround ourselves with those already making remote or blended learning environments work. If we did not have a personal learning network before 2020, I hope that we all have learned just how important this group of support will be for educators of all years of experience. If we have learned anything from 2020, we now know we must find the motivation, take the initiative, seek new solutions, and embrace the tools we have at our fingertips. This year may have revealed unforeseen challenges, but it also afforded us the ability to access new worlds of learning and new and creative ways to teach and engage students.

References

An, Y. (2012). Learner-centered technology integration. Encyclopedia of e-leadership, counseling, and training; 3v (pp. 797-807). Portland: Ringgold Inc. Retrieved from https://libproxy.library.unt.edu/login?url= https://libproxy.library.unt.edu:2165/ docview/919046747?accountid=7113

Elliot, C. (2007). Action Research: Authentic Learning Transforms Student and Teacher Success. Retrieved from https://dspace.sunyconnect.suny.edu/handle/1951/41487

Herrington, J., Reeves, T. C., Oliver, R., & Woo, Y. (2004). Designing authentic activities in web-based courses. Journal of Computing in Higher Education, 16(1), 3-29.

Huang, H., (2002) Toward constructivism for adult learners in online learning environments, British Journal of Educational Technology, 33(1), 27-37.

McCombs, B. (2015). Learner-Centered Online Instruction. New Directions For Teaching And Learning, 2015(144), 57-71. doi: 10.1002/tl.20163

Noonoo, S. (2020). How Long Should a Remote School Day Be? There's No Consensus - EdSurge News. Retrieved from https://www.edsurge.com/news/2020-05-04-how-long-should-a-remote-school-day-be-there-s-no-consensus

Romero, M., & Barberà, E. (2011). Quality of e-learners' time and learning performance beyond quantitative time-on-task. The International Review Of Research In Open And Distributed Learning, 12(5), 125. doi: 10.19173/irrodl.v12i5.999

Rubenstein, G. (2010). Ten tips for personalized learning via technology. Retrieved from https://www.edutopia.org/stw-differentiated-instruction-ten-key-lessons

TISHA PONCIO

Tisha Poncio

Tisha Poncio, M.S. Learning Technologies/Instructional Design, is an energetic and enthusiastic learner, teacher, coach, and empowered educator. Tisha has served in education for the last 20 years. She has led students in the classroom teaching English, Web Design, Graphic Design, Business Computers, Programming, and Broadcast Journalism. She has also led educators and administrators as a digital learning specialist for 12 years. She is a Google Certified Trainer, a Flipgrid Ambassador, an Ed Tech Team Blogger, and was named a finalist in 2018 for Instructional Technology Specialist of the Year in Texas. She has presented at numerous educational technology conferences across the nation and in her home state of Texas speaking about empowering students, teachers, and leaders as well as digital citizenship for all ages. Her biggest accomplishment to date has been the creation of a student-led technology leadership group that helps her present on student voice, empowerment, and the #studentsCANlead movement.

3

SPECIAL EDUCATION IN THE AGE OF COVID-19: HOW TO WIN OVER DYSLEXIA

WINIFRED A. WINSTON (@SOALLCANREAD)

There is no doubt distance learning has been challenging for students with disabilities. However, we know first hand it has been especially challenging for educators to implement Individual Education Plans (IEPs) during this pandemic. Most schools are not equipped with the necessary tools and technology to create a thriving virtual classroom that works for all learners, especially our dyslexic learners who struggle with learning to read, write, and spell. It is estimated that one in five students has dyslexia, yet some students go unidentified in today's classrooms, which is especially frightening in the age of Covid-19.

But first...What does the law say?

According to the United States Department of Education, during Covid closures, state educational agencies (SEAs), local educational agencies (LEAs), and schools "must provide equitable access to comparable opportunities to students with disabilities, tailored to their individual needs, to the maximum extent possible." Schools, and that, of course, means educators, must find ways to provide the supplementary aids and accommodations in the IEP because that's what the team determined the student needed.

Distance learning presents a much bigger challenge than having a reliable Internet connection and an up-to-date functioning device such as a laptop, tablet, or desktop - it includes additional assistive technology such as audiobooks & publications, speech-recognition programs, electronic math worksheets, and alternative keyboards. The use of technology in the virtual classroom creates a unique opportunity for educators to create new and innovative ways for students to continue learning in ways that meet their individual needs.

Google stock images

Educate

Learn all you can about assistive technology and learning disabilities. According to the International Dyslexia Association (IDA), technologies that can be of help to those with dyslexia and other learning disabilities fall primarily into one of two categories: instructional technology (IT) and assistive technology (AT).

For the sake of this piece, I'm going to refer to assistive technology to encompass both. AT is any device, software, or equipment that helps students work around their challenges. Here are some great technology and tools designed to compensate for a student's skills deficit, improve phonic skills, and remedial reading software to help children with dyslexia and other language-based learning disabilities.

- Readworks - Choose leveled reading passages with text to speech
- Storyshares - Graphic novels at various grade levels with text to speech
- VoiceDream - An app with accessibility features for reading books from Bookshare, Gutenberg, and the web
- Rewordify - If a learner needs to have difficult text reworded so that it's easier to understand, from a digital textbook online or from websites
- Unite for Literacy - Provides free access to picture books, narrated in many different languages
- Microsoft OneNote - Immersive reader
- Tar Heel Reader - Books for beginning readers of all ages

There are several options for audiobooks that parents might already be familiar with, such as Audible (fee), Learning Ally (fee), Bookshare (free), and Libby (free).

The use of AT can help students with dyslexia unlock their full potential and foster independence. By addressing the diversity of their needs, AT can also address dyscalculia, dysgraphia, and other learning difficulties such as listening and organization, and memory.

Lastly, there are several factors to consider when evaluating AT products for students. Most importantly, educators should consider the interventions, services, and accommodations outlined in the IEP. Are you providing supplementary aids and accommodations that are aligned with the students' IEP goals? What is the student's comfortability and level with using technology? Contact your school's AT team for further guidance and information, and be sure to review your state's assessment, accessibility, and accommodations policy manual.

Did you know *Microsoft has partnered with MadeByDyslexia to ensure that every teacher around the world is trained in dyslexia awareness, and they have created a FREE dyslexia course for teachers?*

Empower

Arm yourself with knowledge of the various Orton-Gillingham (OG) approaches to reading intervention for children with dyslexia. The OG approach is a direct, explicit, multisensory, structured, sequential, diagnostic, and prescriptive way to teach literacy when reading, writing, and spelling does not come easily to individuals who have dyslexia or other language-based learning disabilities, according to the Orton-Gillingham Academy. It simply is not enough to only know the interventions your school may be using to work with struggling readers, as other interventions may be designed to accommodate distance learning or "homeschooling." Here is a list of programs you should explore further:

- Barton Reading & Spelling
- Pride Reading Program
- Nessy Learning Programme
- Homeschooling with Dyslexia
- Phono-Graphix Reading Company

If you are interested in more formalized training that may count towards professional development, teacher certification, or your local school district may cover the cost, here are a few options to explore:

- Dyslexia for Teachers: Seattle Pacific Continuing Professional Education EDCT 5776.
- Dyslexia, Dysgraphia & Dyscalculia (Post-Master's Certificate): Notre Dame of Maryland University in partnership with Jemicy School
- Dyslexia Certificate: Mount St. Joseph University
- Master of Science, Reading Specialist - Literacy

Leadership: McDaniel College, in partnership with Wilson Reading System.

Did you know *there are 12 Orton-Gillingham Approach Principles? Personalized, multisensory, diagnostic & prescriptive, direct Instruction, systematic phonics, applied linguistics, systematic & structured, sequential, incremental & cumulative, continuous feedback & positive reinforcement, cognitive approach, emotionally sound, and linguistic competence.*

Google stock images

Equip

As a classroom teacher, it's imperative that you practice self-care. I debated about mentioning this, but determined it had to be included.

Too many of our colleagues have particularly high rates of burning out from emotional, mental, and physical exhaustion. You must access tools available to you in your employer benefits, such as Employee Assistance Plan (EAP) and telehealth. Mental and behavioral health is paramount during this pandemic, but it's absolutely necessary in education. There is zero instruction taking place if you are not mentally and emotionally healthy. Education in the age of Covid-19 is challenging, and special education in the age of Covid-19 brings on unique circumstances that only an educator and parent can fully comprehend. Often family and friends who do not do this work can not help. We need to seek professional help and do what's necessary to maintain our mental health. I read online recently an unknown quote I want to share, "If you don't make time for your wellness, you will be forced to make time for your illness." As educators, we must give ourselves some grace.

Did you know *according to the National Center for Education Statistics (NCES), only 19% of public schools and 13% of private schools offered distance learning before Covid-19? With the immediate switch to distance learning, we are not alone.*

In conclusion, I hope these three quick steps provide you with timely and useful information to assist you in implementing special education services to your dyslexic students in the age of Covid-19. Educate, empower, and equip yourself with the technology and structured literacy to win over dyslexia so all can read during the Covid-19 pandemic.

Resources & Further Reading

> AT for Education - Technology, tools, and resources to support reading achievement https://wakelet.com/wake/mi7WyTGXHddyu5DkVE912
>
> Edumatch Snapshot in Education 2019 - Educators, Get Comfortable with the Uncomfortable: Dyslexia
>
> Dyslexia Awareness in Partnership with MadeByDsyexia: Free course for teachers https://www.microsoft.com/en-ca/education/dyslexia-decoded
>
> Independent Teacher Training Programs Accredited by IDA https://dyslexiaida.org/accredited-teaching-training-programs/

International Dyslexia Association (IDA) Overview of Instructional and Assistive Technology: Critical Tools for Students Who Struggle

Microsoft | Educator Center: Special education and accessibility resources for remote learning https://education.microsoft.com/en-us/resource/0c6e9c42

Reading Rockets: Assistive Technology for Kids with Learning Disabilities: An Overview https://www.readingrockets.org/article/assistive-technology-kids-learning-disabilities-overview

10 Mental Health Tips for Teachers During the Covid-19 Pandemic https://everfi.com/blog/k-12/10-ways-educators-can-support-their-mental-health/

US Dept. of Education: Questions and Answers on Providing Services to Children with Disabilities During the Coronavirus Disease 2019 Outbreak (March 2020) https://sites.ed.gov/idea/idea-files/q-and-a-providing-services-to-children-with-disabilities-during-the-coronavirus-disease-2019-outbreak/

University Programs Accredited by IDA
https://dyslexiaida.org/university-programs-accredited-by-ida/

Special Education in the age of Covid-19: How to Win Over Dyslexia

Winifred A. Winston

Winifred A. Winston is a bestselling author, passionate advocate, and enthusiastic speaker. She has worked in education providing career services for more than 10 years. She has worked with non-traditional students, students with disabilities, and adult learners in both high school and in higher education as a career coach and adjunct instructor.

After working as an administrator of a special education school, being a high school teacher in an alternative high school setting, and going through the IEP process in the public school system with her daughter, Winifred quickly realized Black parents lacked access to accurate information about dyslexia interventions and instructional strategies. With established industry contacts and a desire to educate families about dyslexia and the IEP process, Winifred founded Dyslexia Advocation, Inc., to equip parents of children with dyslexia and other language based learning disabilities with the necessary tools to help their kids become successful readers.

WINIFRED A. WINSTON (@SOALLCANREAD)

Winifred is committed to service and accepted the Presidential Appointment as a Selective Service Board Member for the state of Maryland, is a founding National Board Member of Dispelling Dyslexia, and Board Chair of Baltimore City's Special Education Citizen's Advisory Committee. She is a Global Career Development Facilitator (GCDF), holds a Master of Science in Human Resource Development from Towson University and a Bachelor of Science in Mass Communications from the University of North Carolina at Pembroke. Winifred is originally from Brooklyn, New York and lives in Baltimore, Maryland by way of Raeford, North Carolina.

4

LEARNING HOW TO TEACH REMOTELY

KRISTEN KOPPERS, NBCT

There are five challenges with remote learning that are important in learning how to teach as an educator in 2020.

Remote learning definitely has its challenges with parents, students, and teachers. As eLearning was an emergency requirement in the spring, many of us had no idea of what we were doing as the State Board of Education practically ended the year in December of the previous year. Only two months into the spring semester, a lot of pressure was put on teachers to motivate students during this time; very little was expected, making it almost impossible to motivate students who did not want to be motivated.

As changes were made, many schools focused on remote or hybrid learning for the fall. As stated in my first sentence, remote learning had its challenges. The challenges began in July when schools were starting to construct plans for the new year. No matter what decision was made, teachers knew that all stakeholders would not be comfortable with the outcome.

As a secondary education teacher, I knew that teaching remotely, after making the transition from face to face to eLearning to remote learning, would create an interruption in a student's ability to learn. While it is not impossible to learn remotely, some believe that the challenges outweigh the benefits.

I am entering my nineteenth year at my current school with over twenty years in education. Instead of returning to my classroom and arranging the desks to ensure mobility around the classroom, I'll be preparing an area within my house ready to begin the school year.

Challenge #1 - Meeting Students

One of the greatest challenges that was hard to overcome was physically seeing my students face to face. Even though I'm able to virtually see them, I'm not able to make the connections that I would by seeing them in class. Within just a few days, I was able to connect with my students virtually. However, it was not the same. The fact that remote learning created a barrier between my students and me eventually will have its disadvantages. Not only is it difficult to "meet" the students virtually, but holding discussions in class becomes difficult virtually. It's not the conversations that are difficult but the students' interactions that are lost. After a week of live virtual remote learning, my students admitted that they wanted to be in class instead of at their home in class.

Challenge #2 - Delivering Content

I never thought about how easy it was to deliver content to my students with ease before the pandemic. The opportunity to explain in detail the lesson, whether it was verbally or not, by using a dry erase board made it easy for students to take notes from the board, for teachers to write down keywords, and for students to write on the board during lessons and activities—just one day of working online uncovered complications for delivering content. While presenting my lesson, the audio was not playing for students, some parts of the PowerPoint were not playing correctly, and there were also other issues. Despite some platforms having the option to use a whiteboard, it's not as easy as it seems without purchasing extra applications or computer add-ons.

Challenge #3 - Dealing with Change

Certain changes make people feel an urge to resist them. Many are hesitant to accept change as it means to accept admitting their fears. But change can be a healthy way to acknowledge opportunity. However, the fear of remote learning comes from the unknown. Because we cannot know the outcome of remote learning methods, we fear students won't receive the same education. While we may not like change, we need to look at the positive side of adjusting to a new schedule. I, for one, do not like dramatic changes as it creates unneeded anxiety in me to try and figure out alternative plans. It's not the change that creates anxiety but the domino effect that does. While teaching (and learning) from home is the current situation for many schools across the nation, it's better to focus on how the change can benefit the students.

Challenge #4 - Problem with Online Learning

With remote learning, students are required to log into their learning platform at certain times during the day. These times will correspond with "class periods" for the students. The problem lies with parents who cannot be home to meet these requirements, especially for elementary school-age children. With many schools not returning to in-person instruction, many have taken the option to homeschool to set their own schedule. Even with parents who choose to stay home, difficulties can arise with meeting times due to connectivity problems.

Challenge #5 - Disengaged Students

I wish I had a magic wand to engage all students. As an educator, motivating disengaged students is a challenge for us all. Trying to engage students during in-person instruction is easier said than done, but it can be done. However, attempting to engage students virtually is harder. The best way to engage students through remote learning is to continuously acknowledge them by including them during the lesson. Students will often turn off their camera or move it upwards to look at the ceiling. There were many times that students did not have a camera on at all. And while I understand that some cannot have a camera on them for various reasons, they understand it needs to be on so that I can acknowledge them. What I started doing to ensure students were engaged was to create a poll for all students to answer. This helped me see who was paying attention and who needed to be redirected. Another way to ensure students were engaged was to 'cold call' them by creating a digital randomizer. There are many ways to engage students who may not be fully invested in a lesson. But most importantly, it's best to create that connection with the students first before implementing any strategies.

To continue engaging students throughout the semester, I've focused on creating ice-breakers that were more engaging than disengaged.

These five challenges will not define who we are as educators, students, and parents. These five challenges are only a fraction of changes that need to be made throughout the year to help our students succeed and learn how to conform to these changes.

Kristen Koppers, NBCT

Kristen Koppers is a National Board Certified Teacher in English. She is a blogger, presenter, a self-published author, and a high school educator as well as an adjunct professor at a local junior college. She has been teaching for twenty years and is currently teaching high school English in Illinois holding a Master of Arts degree in English and a Master of Arts degree in Education Administration. Kristen is the author of *Differentiated Instruction in the Teacher Profession* (2019) and *The Perfect Puppy* (2020). She shares her ideas of how to use Differentiated Instruction inside the classroom. As an educator, it is important to find innovative ways to meet the needs of students. Kristen is often on Twitter (@Mrs_Koppers) participating in chats and collaborating with other educators.
#DITeaching #ThePerfectPuppyEdu
https://kristenkoppers.wixsite.com/koppers

5

REFLECTION TIP #12

WHAT PRACTICES ARE YOU INTEGRATING INTO YOUR
BLENDED LEARNING CLASSROOM?

JAMI FOWLER-WHITE, NBCT

Blended Learning has many connotations which presents educators with the unique opportunity to be innovative as they build the model that works best in their classroom.

If we teach today as we taught yesterday, we rob our children of tomorrow.

— JOHN DEWEY

Have you ever felt as if you were behind the curve when it comes to figuring out the right balance between teacher-directed instruction, student-centered learning, and technology integration? If so, you are not alone. Many schools are moving towards implementing the Blended Learning model of instruction. This type of disruptive innovation creates uneasiness among many educators. Most of us prefer what is commonly referred to as sustained innovation. Sustained innovation means holding on to the existing state of education by continuing to teach the same way that we always have. In contrast, disruptive innovation is acquiring novel ideas, accepting new technologies, and executing brand-new initiatives and representations for instruction. The move of many school districts towards implementing a Blended Learning model of instruction can be considered disruptive innovation.

Society today makes it possible for children to interact with technology from an early age. These opportunities afford children the experience of being able to grow and learn as new types of technology are developed. By doing this our children will develop technological skills naturally which will help them grow up to be successful technologically literate citizens (Truitt, 2016). When educators hold on to the existing state of education by continuing to deliver instruction using the same methodology instead of changing as new technology is established, teachers are sustaining innovation. In order to prepare students for an ever-changing world and jobs that we can only imagine, they need educators who embrace the disruptive innovation of the Blended Learning models by being willing to acquire new ideas, accept new technologies, and implement new initiatives and methods for instruction.

In the wake of the Coronavirus Pandemic, it is essential for educators to rethink how they view blended learning and work to incorporate routines and procedures to ensure continuity of learning for all students. During this transitional period in education, there is a need to infuse the person-to-person interactions of traditional educational settings with developing technological innovations. The challenge with this type of shift in education is the lack of literature to guide teachers and school leaders through this process. Everyone needs guidance and support when incorporating new practices. When looking for resources on Blended Learning, teachers should choose resources that address the instructional techniques, tips for working with students, and include suggested management strategies (Truitt, 2016).

Reflection Tip #12

Blended learning has several monikers of which, "hybrid learning, mixed-mode learning, and web-enhanced learning" (Picciano, 2010, p. 3) are the most popular. For the purposes of this chapter, blended learning is defined as the "thoughtful fusion of face-to-face and online learning experiences" (Garrison & Vaughan, 2008, p.5). In the case of educators, it is important to understand that things constantly change in education, so they must remain flexible and willing to learn as much as possible about the new innovations.

In their research, Osguthorpe and Graham (2003) describe three main elements of a Blended Learning model. A formal education program in which a student learns at least in part through online learning, with some element of personalized learning is the first element. Personalized learning is not differentiated learning. In essence, personalized learning equates to a student having some control over the time, place, path, and/or pace of their learning. The second element requires a portion of the learning takes place in a supervised brick-and-mortar location away from home. Third, the modalities along each student's learning path within a course or subject are connected to an integrated learning experience. Learners use one or a combination of modalities to receive and process new information. These modalities include kinesthetic (moving), tactile (touching), auditory (hearing), and visual (seeing) learning. With these three things in mind, it is vital for each educator to carefully think about the characteristics of each model of blended learning and choose components that are the most appropriate for their learning environment and students.

Several models fall under the Blended Learning umbrella. In this chapter, five (Rotation, A La Carte, Enriched Virtual, and Flex Model) will be highlighted and information on additional models for use in either tradition or Career and Technical school environments can be found at the end of the chapter. As you read, think about the premise behind each model and keep a list of the components that you would like to incorporate into your current classroom practices. Let's dive in.

Rotation Model

One of the more commonly known models is the rotation model. In this model, students rotate through academic learning stations on a fixed schedule or as determined by the teacher. The most important criteria for this model is that at least one of the academic stations must integrate an online component. Unlike the other blended learning models, students do not have to have access to technology outside of school to implement it. When adopting the station rotation model, teachers should be aware that the expectation is for students to spend 50-75% of their time in teacher-led instruction or independent practice that is combined with 25-50% of student's time spent learning online. One benefit to this model is that teachers can differentiate the way content is presented to students, how information is delivered to students, and the methods students use to demonstrate mastery of the lesson content (Govindaraj & Silverajah, 2017). Although this model allows for differentiation, the teacher remains in control of learning by determining the interval of time students spend at each station and provide students with signals indicating which stations they will visit as well as when they are allowed to move to each station. There are different styles of the rotation model. The most notable are the flipped classroom, station rotation, and lab rotation.

A. Flipped Classroom

Flipped classrooms reverse the traditional relationship between class time and homework. In this model, students learn at home via online coursework and lectures. Utilizing this model, the teacher uses class time for teacher-guided practice or project-based learning versus delivering traditional direct instruction or lectures. Students enter the classroom with background knowledge and spend time during school applying what they learned at home. The flipped model allows for a more personalized approach to teaching and learning (Ayobl et al., 2019). This model requires one-to-one devices for students, has minimal disruption to a classroom's layout, and would not require teachers or schools to make modifications within the school schedule. When considering this model, make sure that students have access to the internet and institute strict protocols that will keep students accountable for completing learning at home.

B. Station Rotation

Station rotation is a model that is implemented completely within the school setting. When executing this model, teachers create several different stations in the classroom for students to rotate through. As with the other rotation models, at least one of the stations would include technology of some kind and can include any type of learning modality that the teacher chooses. After creating the learning stations, the teacher creates a schedule and at a specific increment of time signals to students that it is time to move to the next station. The teacher is in complete control of the type of activities that students complete as well as when students will visit each academic station. If you are considering using this model, be sure to create management protocols to hold students accountable for assignments at each station and ensure that students can efficiently move between the stations.

C. Lab Rotation

Lab rotation is similar to station rotation in that this model, it also takes place solely within the school day. The teacher determines one online academic station for students to rotate through and the amount of time that students will spend at this station. The major difference between the station rotation and the lab rotation is that students move to a computer lab and spend time working through an online curriculum for part of the school day instead of completing all stations within one classroom setting.

To help you picture what this might look like inside of your classroom, as the teacher you would teach a lesson to your students in their classroom. Once students understand the skill that you are teaching, your students would then move to a computer lab to complete online coursework to apply what they have learned. While some of the students are completing work in the computer lab, you would have the opportunity to pull out small groups of students to provide differentiated, personalized instruction. When beginning to implement a blended learning model, this one is the most similar to the traditional instructional model in that the teacher teaches her lesson as usual. Then students move to a lab that is in many cases supported by a teacher assistant (Spiro, 2020). This model is the easiest to implement if you are teaching at a school that does not have enough devices for every classroom.

Flex Model

Like the Station Rotation Model, students also rotate through learning stations. However, the Flex Model allows students to move fluidly through stations based on their academic needs and not a set schedule. Online learning is the backbone of student learning in a Flex model. Teachers provide support and instruction on a flexible, as needed, basis while students work through course curriculum and content at their own pace. This model can give students a high degree of control over their learning (Osguthorpe et al., 2003). When using this model, a teacher gives students several choices of learning tasks to complete. These tasks could be within a choice board, in lists with specific categories, or available to students on an online document which allows students to schedule how they will spend their time during the school day. The Flex model helps to build student agency and affords teachers more time to personalize student feedback and support student progress. Before beginning this model, teachers should be aware that this model takes up a lot of space. There will need to be a designated area set aside for students to move to as they complete each academic task that is listed on student's choice boards. For example, if students can choose between ten different tasks. Teachers will need to have areas of all 10 tasks, because there is a possibility that students will be working in any of the ten areas simultaneously throughout the day or week.

A la Carte Model

The A la Carte model is set up so that students complete one or more courses completely online while taking other courses in a face-to-face setting with teachers. This model is especially beneficial for offering personalized, individual instruction on a student-by-student basis. If you are considering using this model, be sure to determine whether your student's learning modalities will hinder their ability to learn effectively in an entirely virtual setting. Many high schools find this model particularly enticing as it allows for students to complete elective classes in a study hall or at home, minimizes the amount of instructors needed for those classes, and can be monitored through the use of e-mail or the online courses themselves.

Enriched Virtual Model

The enriched virtual model is set up so that students learn completely online. In this model, students learn remotely instead of at a brick and mortar building. Teachers instruct students at various times throughout the week, but their face-to-face sessions with students do not take place every day. This model provides students with the flexibility of creating their own learning schedules. Teachers have time to work on multiple campuses. Since learning is completely online, teachers can also provide instruction to more students than they could within the brick-and-mortar school setting. This model requires drastic schedule modifications for teachers, parents, and students as it is the furthest alteration from the traditional school model. In addition to the schedule modifications, students will also need access to both their own device and stable internet access at their homes. Although this model is completely virtual, some teachers and schools slightly modify this model and offer in-person assistance to students who need it.

Stop, Think, and Write: You have read an overview of five types of Blended Learning models, follow the link to read about other formats educators could use to structure blended learning. As you read, complete as least one of these two tasks:

- Determine which model is the most advantageous. Create a T-chart to create a list of the advantages and shortcomings for each model. Review your notes to determine which model would be best to implement.
- Create your own model: List the qualities that most resonate with you with all of the models as a whole you could implement in your classroom to disrupt your instructional practices and move towards a more blended learning model.

Reflection Tip #12

Implementing a Blended Learning Model

Once the decision is made to incorporate a blended learning model in your classroom it is critical to craft a plan for this change. This plan should include systems and processes for use during both in-person and virtual learning instruction. Routines and procedures will help provide structure and continuity of instruction during periods of intermittent closures, ensure students receive personalized learning, and keep the focus on continuous academic growth of students.

When adopting the blended learning model, consider the following when planning in-person classroom procedures and routines:

1. **Curriculum & Overall Goals**: Examine your curriculum to determine what you will be teaching, the objectives of your lessons, and the best approach to take to help students master the content standards. Once you have determined these things, choose a blended learning model that will best fit your students needs.
2. **Teaching & Content Knowledge are Key**: Based on the curriculum and lesson objectives, determine which teaching strategies and methods will work best with the blended learning model that you chose. To implement the Blended Learning model, teachers must have strong content knowledge. How well do you understand the content that you are teaching students?
3. **Technology & Platforms Matters**: Do you have enough technology to implement the blended learning model that you selected? Have you researched platforms that allow students to learn asynchronously? Are they compatible with other platforms that have been adopted by your district? Are there any restricted software that you should

be aware of within your school district? How long will it take for you to prepare the online curriculum that students will be learning?

4. **Inclement Weather/Pandemic**: Are there any procedures that need to be taught to ensure continuity if there is a sudden closure due to snow, a tornado, or another natural disaster?

What will collaboration routines look like in an environment that requires social distancing? Have you reviewed the Center for Disease Control (CDC) guidelines or your school's emergency plan? Reviewing these guidelines and plans will help you determine many of the routines and procedures that you will need to focus on within the first few weeks of school.

Systems and Routines: How will you redesign the layout of your classroom? Will you institute the same procedures as last year? How will you teach these methods to the students? Is there anything that needs to be revised?

Systems and processes for the online portion of your blended learning model must also be well thought out. There are a variety of programs and platforms available to teachers to consider – Zoom, Google Classroom, ClassDojo, are just a few. Another consideration includes the availability of other online applications, either district mandated, or teacher selected, to be used for turning in assignments, checking for understanding, or enhancing lessons. With all of these, it is critical each is researched carefully and implemented together in a manner that does not frustrate your students. A last caution – take into consideration that all students will not have the same level of connectivity at home – not doing so can adversely affect student achievement and widen the learning gap.

Reflection Tip #12

Questions to ask when considering the online component of Blended Learning:

1. **The Platform**: Which one will you use? Which tools or features does the platform offer?
2. **Classroom Ground Rules**: What will your classroom protocols be?
3. **Safety/Security**: Will you assign a code/password? Will students enter through a waiting room? If so, will students use the same process to enter each day?
4. **Instructional Format**: How long will you spend giving direct instruction to students? How will you incorporate small group instruction? Will you be able to find innovative ways for students to collaborate with each other? How will you personalize learning for each student? How will you balance asynchronous and synchronous learning opportunities for students?
5. **E.M.P.O.W.E.R Feedback™**: How will you ensure that students receive E.M.P.O.W.E.R Feedback™ that will help them grow and learn? As a reminder, the E.M.P.O.W.E.R Feedback framework was introduced in Chapter 6 of Volume #1 of Educator Reflection Tips: How often do you reflect on your practice? This framework outlines seven steps that teachers could implement which will empower students to take ownership for their own learning.

If you need additional information, a few resources are included below to help you continue to grow and learn about this topic. There are also additional resources on my blog, DigitalPD4You, specifically Reflection Tips #50-73. These Reflection Tips dig deeper into all of these questions, are accompanied by examples of what classrooms around the world look like, and provide additional resources to help you strengthen your knowledge of blended learning instructional models that other schools around the world are implementing.

Additional resources to conduct further research

Edutopia: Article and Implementation Video
https://www.edutopia.org/article/blended-learning-built-teacher-expertise

Khan Academy (Model Descriptions)
https://www.khanacademy.org/partner-content/ssf-cci/sscc-intro-blended-learning/sscc-blended-learning-models/v/sscc-blended-4models

Benefits of Each Blended Learning Model:
https://blog.edmentum.com/talking-ed-which-blended-learning-model-right-you

E-School News
https://www.eschoolnews.com/2020/06/15/the-blended-learning-models-that-can-help-schools-reopen/61b87b52511b&pf_rd_r=TJTQZD18V2GXMT21W5PD&psc=1&refRID=TJTQZD18V2GXMT21W5PD

Reflection Tip #12

DigitalPD4YOU.com
Educator Reflection Tip #12
What practices are you integrating into your Blended Learning Classroom?

What is Blended Learning?

Many schools are moving towards implementing Blended Learning models of instruction. This disruptive innovation usually includes the following components:

- In-person learning experiences
- Online learning experiences
- Usually includes some personalized learning for students
- Student-centered learning

Strategy #1

Blended Learning Models

There are more than twelve different combinations of Blended Learning models. Here are a few that you might consider using in your classroom:

- Station Rotation
- Flipped Classroom
- Flex model
- Lab rotation
- Remote
- Self-Directed
- Mastery-Based
- Project-Based

Strategy #2

Planning for In-person learning experiences

Educators should prepare for the following when teaching in traditional settings:

- What is your plan for assessing students academic needs?
- Which systems and routines and behavior expectations will you implement?
- How you will meet students social/emotional needs?
- Have you included time to prepare students for inclement weather/pandemic emergency school closures?
- What will your process for collaboration look like?

Strategy #3

Planning for online learning experiences

Educators should prepare for the following when teaching planning remote learning experiences for students:

- Which platform(s) will you use? Are all the platforms you are using compatible?
- What norms or expectations will you implement?
- How will you provide feedback to students?
- How will students interact with their peers?
- What other systems and routines will you need to implement to minimize disruptions to instruction?
- How will you meet individual students social and emotional needs?

Strategy #4

Copyright © 2020 Jami Fowler-White, NBCT. All rights reserved
Individual infographics are available for download at https://www.DigitalPD4you.com

REFERENCES

Ayobl, N., Abd Halim, N., Zulkifli, N.., Zaid, N., Mokhtar, M. (2019). Overview of blended learning: The effect of station rotation model on students' achievement. *Journal of Critical Review.* 7(6): 320-326. DOI: http://dx.doi.org/10.31838/jcr.07.06.56

Edmentum. (2016). Blended Learning: Fundamentals of the Planning Process. Retrieved on September 19. 2020 from https://blog.edmentum.com/talking-ed-which-blended-learning-model-right-you.

Garrison, D.R., & Vaughan, N.D. (2008). Blended Learning in Higher Education: Framework, Principles and Guidelines. San Francisco: Jossey-Bass.

Govindaraj, A. & Silverajah Giita, V. (2017). Blending Flipped Classroom and Station Rotation Models in Enhancing Students' Learning of Physics. 73-78. 10.1145/3175536.3175543.

Osguthorpe, R.T. & Graham, C.R. (2003). Blended Learning Environments: Definitions and Directions. *Quarterly Review of Distance Education, 4*(3), 227. Retrieved July 12, 2020 from https://www.learntechlib.org/p/97576/.

Smith, K., & Hill, J. (2018). Defining the nature of blended learning through its depiction in current research. Higher Education Research and Development. DOI: 10.1080/07294360.2018.1517732

Spiro, K. (2020). Lab Rotation Model. Retrieved on September 19. 2020 from https://www.easygenerator.com/en/blog/blended-learning/lab-rotation-model.

Truitt, A. (2016). A Case Study of the Station Rotation Blended Learning Model in a Third Grade Classroom (Doctoral Dissertation). University of Northern Colorado.

Tucker, C. (2018). 10 tips for teachers using the station-rotation model. Retrieved on 9/11/2020 from https://catlintucker.com/2018/09/10-tips-station-rotation-model/

Infographics were created using the Poster My Wall Premium Software and Creative Common photos from Depositphotos and DigitalPD4You.

Reflection Tip #12

Jami Fowler-White, NBCT

Jami Fowler-White is an Educational Specialist who began her career as an elementary school teacher at the age of 21. She spent ten years molding and educating young minds, earned National Board Certification in the area of Middle Childhood Generalist, and served as the Technology Coordinator for her school. From there she went on to spend the next nine years, as a Title I Instructional/Professional Development Coach were her primary role was to help teachers strengthen their knowledge of content pedagogy and research-based instructional strategies which could be used to increase student achievement. During this time, she also helped to train other Instructional Coaches within her district, served as a Tennessee Candidate Support Provider and mentor to National Board Teaching Certification First-Time and Renewal Candidates in her state, and became a charter member of the Tennessee Core Advocate Network in the area of Foundational Literacy. After serving as an Instructional Coach, Mrs. Fowler-White was promoted to the role of Assistant Principal at her school, went on to renew her National Board Teaching Certification, is currently serving as a mentor to National Board Teaching Certification candidates across the United States, and is a charter member of the of the National Board Network of Accomplished Minorities. Additionally, Mrs. Fowler-White is also a proud member of Delta Sigma Theta Sorority, Incorporated. Mrs. Fowler-White currently serves as an Assistant Principal in Shelby County Schools in Tennessee. If you are interested in reading other material written by Mrs. Fowler-White, she published a book entitled, Educator Reflection Tips: How often do you reflect on your practice and publishes a blog and podcast called Digital PD 4 You.

6

REMOTE PD IS LIKE A 24 HOUR EDCAMP

BRUCE REICHER

This is the best time ever for educator PD

Remote PD Is Like a 24 Hour Global Edcamp

Have you ever been to an Edcamp? An Edcamp is an unconference where all the educators who attend the conference can become presenters. The schedule is built on a board, and you can pick and choose the sessions you want to attend. The vibe at an Edcamp is totally different than your normal conference. There is no keynote speaker that everyone attending needs to listen to. The educators who attend the Edcamp are attending to share, learn, and network with each other. All educators at an Edcamp want to be there!

Since the pandemic in March, there have been no in-person Edcamps, but I believe all remote PD is like a 24-hour global Edcamp. All educators like to share with each other, and everyone is home with remote learning. This is the perfect storm for amazing authentic PD. Over the past six months, here is the PD I've been able to go to and the connections I've made with other educators.

One of my favorite places to learn has been the Global GEG and the state GEG's. A GEG is a Google Education Group, and its mission is to teach, share, and learn from each other. During the pandemic, I was able to join the Global GEG weekly groups that addressed educators' SEL and wellness. It was amazing to me that I could join a group that included members from all over the United States, England, Canada, and many more countries. I was able to connect on a personal level with the 20 or fewer educators who were in the Google Meet. I would encourage every educator to join their state GEG and check out the Global GEG events. They have amazing online training that is FREE.

This past summer, there were more free conferences you could attend than time in a day. I tried to keep my digital balance but did attend many local, state, and international conferences. I learned to always check the time zones as all these conferences were in different locations. My favorites this summer were the WeVideo conference, the #2020ChangeMakerConference, and the Microsoft CUE conference.

Remote PD also allowed me to join #CoffeeEdus, located two hours from my house. A CoffeeEdu before the pandemic took place at a local coffee place where educators would meet for an hour and exchange ideas. Once this terrific chat went online with Zoom, I was now able to attend the weekly Sunday conversation and connect with educators from around my state of New Jersey. This group has covered important topics of remote learning, school reopening, racism, and student equity. I have learned so much from these educators, and I have remote PD to thank.

My two 24/7 learning centers are called Facebook and Twitter. I can go on and learn and connect with educators at any time of the day or night. This has been the most effective PD I've done in my 25 years as an educator. I've been able to connect with educators worldwide, and now I have an amazing PLN.

Finally, my goal for this summer was to go to as many conferences as possible and promote our book, Scripted. Due to the pandemic, I was not able to go to any conference in person, but I was able to send a DM (Direct Message) to 15 podcasts and book myself and my co-authors Paula Neidlinger and Randall Tomes on 13 different shows. I am so thankful we could tell our story and share our book's premise that everyone can create media. Since I live in New Jersey, and Paula and Randy live in Indiana, there is no way we would be able to attend 13 different conferences together. With remote learning, we could connect with so many amazing educators who have helped us tell our story. Every educator is going through this pandemic differently, but I would suggest every educator reach out on social media and attend as many online conferences as you can. The authors of our book Scripted connected five years ago, and now we have a book! You never know where these online connections are going to take you.

BRUCE REICHER

Bruce Reicher

Bruce Reicher has been an educator for 25 years. The past 14 years he's been a middle school technology teacher in New Jersey. He's also a Dad, Husband, Author, Technology Teacher. State presenter & BOE member. Wakelet Ambassador, Brainpop CBE, Google Certified Level 1&2. @icodeinschool Codesters & @Wevideo Ambassador Knick & Met Fan, Reicher is also a Proud member of the local board of education. He co-authored the *Scripted - An Educator's Guide To Media In The Classroom* with Paula Neidlinger and Randall Tomes came out on August 11, 2020.

7

LET'S LEARN OUTSIDE

MARIE K. MCCUMBER

In the time of Covid teaching, we need to get our students outside for their social, emotional, and academic well-being.

Walk into my classroom, and it will look quite different from the year before. Desks are spaced out as far as I can make them in an arch across the room. I couldn't bring myself to do rows. My students last year were arranged either in one large group or two smaller groups. Each desk has a clear, plastic tri-fold on top. My half-circle group table has become a storage area for all the cleaning supplies I need, as well as a nice way to lay everything out for the day. I now use a portable, standing desk so that I can go to each student in their space. They shouldn't leave their space.

Last year, we had flexible seating with large pillows, wobble stools, floor seats, bean bag chairs, ball chairs, rolling chairs, and regular desk chairs. The children would switch out their seating throughout the day as their bodies or the activity needed. This year, they have to pick their seat and stay with it for the entire day. There simply isn't time in the day to sanitize seats between use.

I am grateful to have my students in a physical space again. I missed them terribly. We have shortened days and a shortened week. I am with my students through specials and lunch. Most of that time, they are at their desks, behind their plastic walls, wearing masks. Even our playground time is tightly scheduled and regimented. My class of students who love to play collaboratively and love to give and receive hugs is now not permitted to leave their space without permission. They must only travel a certain way, and only as long as everyone else is seated. I understand the necessary restrictions, but they make me sad.

However, when we are outside, all of this changes. The physical walls and the invisible walls built by rules come down. They spread out as far as they can; they move, they walk, they run, they yell. They do all the things that their bodies need. They are clearly happier and more relaxed.

I have always been a huge advocate for outdoor learning. I started a small class of forest school students when I worked at a private school. I tried at the public school; however, they would only permit me a two-week camp in the summer. Being outside lends itself to so many benefits now that we have so many safety restrictions imposed on us inside the classroom walls. We have space to spread out not only six feet, but as far as we can go and still hear each other. We can take off the masks. We can move beyond our own spaces and even change those spaces when needed: no sanitation needed. It's liberating.

I think now, more than ever, we need to advocate for getting kids outside during the school day. This is a stressful, sometimes fearful time for our children. Taking away the walls and giving them some normalcy will help our students' emotional and social development. Besides the already-existing academic and therapeutic benefits, outdoor learning will allow our children to continue to be kids in a time where it can be really hard to do so.

Marie K. McCumber

Marie McCumber began her degree in the Education of the Deaf and Hard-of-Hearing from Bowling Green State University. After taking a break to live in Germany for 3 years with her then-husband and the Air Force, she finished her degree at Ashland University in Early Childhood Intervention. She has worked as a multiple disabilities and low-incidence teacher in both public and private schools always pushing for students to have authentic inclusion in the classroom.

When she worked for Discovery School in Mansfield, Ohio, she designed and ran a 5-week outdoor school in the woods. Children practiced conflict management, literacy through imaginative play, storytelling, nature journaling, and science through building structures and observing wildlife, including the life cycle of the cicada.

She went back to complete more schooling and earned her license to teach students with visual impairments through the Ohio State University. She now works as an Elementary Teacher at the Ohio State School for the Blind, where she is working with administration to create authentic outdoor learning spaces for preschool- through high school-aged students. She will begin work on her Masters in Leadership in Technology through Baldwin Wallace college in the spring.

She loves to write and has published one book, *My Name is Not Jamie*, which is based on a true story from her time working in a Preschool for Children with Disabilities on Vogelweh Air Force Base.

Marie lives in Columbus, Ohio with her two awesome children, her boyfriend, his two sons, and their puppy, Addie. She loves to be outside camping, hiking, fishing, bike-riding, and gardening. She and her boyfriend also cook and bake together, and have begun a podcast called *Cooking Blind* where they talk about how to cook, bake, grill, and smoke when you have a visual impairment.

8

THE POWER OF REPRESENTATION

ALEXES M. TERRY

So I am sitting here listening to Nipsey Hussle as I write. I always listen to Nipsey Hussle when I write, but that's not the point of this chapter. Well, at least not at the moment. Early this morning, I had a coffee and convo with a friend while discussing what's next for me and TwistED Teaching after releasing *REAL LOVE: Strategies for Reaching Students When They See No Way Out*. During this conversation, I shared with her where TwistED Teaching came from and how I started my consultant work blogging (if that's what you want to call it). She asked what happened to my blog, and, like my blog, I had nothing left to say, so I stopped (well before I even got started).

Two things people always find shocking about me are that I hate writing, and I'm not too fond of public speaking. Yeah, I know I wrote a whole book. And, I'll never shy away from presenting or chatting on a live stream or podcast. Still, when I think about writing or talking in a public manner, anxiety fills my body and cripples anything that led me to believe that someone would care about what I have to say. No matter what was on my heart or mind, I would not let it out because... for what? So, I stopped blogging and started putting my heart, soul, and passion back into my journal, idea book, and sticky notes (yeah, I'm that sticky note teacher). I don't know where I got the courage to write *REAL LOVE*. All I can think about is, "BUT GOD!" God knew I had a story to tell, and he lit a fire in me to write because I wouldn't have done it other than that. Where does this fear come from, though?

Growing up in South Central Los Angeles and being educated in the LAUSD, I did not see many representations of Black women from the hood writing or speaking on a public level. We had stories and stuff to say but no spaces to share those stories, or at least spaces that I knew existed. Hip Hop was there, and there were women like YoYo and Rage who were rapping about what it was like growing up in South Central. Still, I wouldn't understand how they were using their platform to share their truth until later in life. I did not know about great women like Angela Davis until I attended a Historically Black College (shout out to GramFam). The message sent to me through schooling was that Black women from the hood are not writers, speakers, and we don't have anything to say that other people would listen to and be inspired from. In *REAL LOVE*, I talked about the confidence that came from participating in Lion's Club speech contest, and if you've read *REAL LOVE*, you're probably wondering how I got to that point. Her name is Sister Souljah. Like many young girls growing up in the early 2000s, I got my hands on a copy of *The Coldest Winter Ever,* and it was life-changing. When I thought about Black women from the hood, I did not think they were writers because nobody wanted to hear about what's happening in the hood. Sister Souljah proved that to be wrong, and she had me hooked. She had me inspired. She helped me see and understand Black women and how they were sharing their stories in a whole new way. In her work, I saw me. I saw what I could do. I saw mattering in my words and stories. My school--as a collective organization--did not show this to me. Sister Souljah showed me that my body, culture, identity, hood, and voice mattered when the education system said otherwise. To be honest, she made me want to talk my "ish," but that was still hard when I was made to feel like I had nothing important to say.

The Coldest Winter Ever took me on this journey to find voices that looked like mine and those whose stories sounded like mine. *A Rose That Grew From Concrete.* Tupac. Life-changing. #RepresentationMatters. I hated writing, but I often used poetry to share my heart. When a teacher used Tupac to teach poetry, like TCWE, it meant something to me. Every kid growing up in L.A. knew who Tupac the rapper was, but to see him as a poet…#representationmatters. To see his work being compared to Shakespeare. #representationmatters. To hear him sharing what it was like growing up in the hood #representationmatters. *Dear Momma,* that was MY story. Sister Souljah's stories matter. Tupac's stories matter. My stories matter. Black students in the hood, their stories matter!

I know I am probably jumping all over the place with this story, but so what *insert shrug.* I'm tired of being silenced and crippled by all the formalities. My job is not to write perfect blogs, stories, posts, or use all the academic language out there. I need to share my voice because it matters, and my students need to see someone like them doing things that our society shows them they can't do or are not supposed to do. Offering our students people who look like them and come from physical and broader communities similar to their own, doing things they've been explicitly or implicitly excluded from, is a must if we will change their experiences with schooling in urban spaces. Students need to see positive representations of themselves in all aspects of our schools because it is empowering and communicates to them all they can do in life. If we want to change the experiences they have with learning, change what they are learning! It's that simple. Many students do not perform at their fullest potential because we have sent a message to them that has stifled and crippled them. Why would I write if what I have to say is not going to be valued? Why would I want to do math if I have never seen anyone who looks like me or come from my hood to use math in a way you are trying to teach me? Why would science matter if what you are using to teach me sends a message that I am not a scientist? "Naw, that ain't for me." "People like me don't do that." "We don't do that where I come from." Our students don't say that because that's what they believe...they say that because that's what we've shown them. That has to change.

When I write or do anything outside of my comfort zone, I listen to Nipsey Hussle. His hood was my hood--literally. The streets I grew up on were the streets he once hanged and banged on. Nipsey The Great he will always be. His lyrics are my truth, and listening to his work takes me back to 105th street. His hustle and stories took him to the top of the Billboard charts, attending the Grammys, changing schools, and opening businesses that would give back to his community. His words are raw, real, and a truth that some are uncomfortable hearing. But I need to hear them. When I feel like my voice does not matter or no one cares about what I have to say, that all changes and confidence comes from the voice of someone who knows what it's like to feel crippled and silenced by the environment that surrounds them—his #representationmatters. So, I will write and share my truth because my voice and stories need to be shared and heard. Because I know the power of representation, I want my students to see me doing what others have excluded them from being because their #representationmatters.

The Power of Representation

Alexes M. Terry (@twstedteaching)

Alexes M. Terry is a wife, mom, educator, and lead consultant at TwistED Teaching Educational Consulting Company. She is the author of *REAL LOVE: Strategies for Reaching Students When They See No Way* and lives each day to transform the educational experiences of students in urban schools.

Alexes's book, *REAL LOVE,* uses her personal story and professional experiences to provide educators with engaging, relevant, and practical strategies on how to educate, connect with, and transforms the lives of students in urban schools who see no way out of the conditions that surround them. You can purchase *REAL LOVE* at bit.ly/realloveedu

9
THE WORK IN BECOMING AN ANTI-RACIST EDUCATOR

MELODY MCALLISTER

White Educators: Your Silence Is Your Complicity

Amid a pandemic, a time when many educators are already feeling the turmoil of crisis/remote teaching and students are feeling alienated even more, we are now also experiencing a time where police brutality against Black men and women can't be ignored as it has been for years in White society. We've seen the murders of innocent People of Color by the very people who have sworn to protect ALL of us. White educators with large platforms are finally feeling the pressure to take a stand when they've never felt obligated to do so in the past. The message is clear, "Your silence says everything we need to know." And that silent message is not a positive one, but a message full of complicity, or the willingness to go on with the status quo. But we also see those who, when they finally say something, may still be canceled on our social media. Whether your feelings are hurt or you feel empowered for the first time, if you have pledged your commitment to ending systemic racism in our public schools and public institutions in the light of glaring reality, your journey will not be an easy one.

Welcome to white guilt. When you finally realize your part in the perpetuation of systemic racism, shame and guilt are mountains you aren't prepared to climb. This is normal. So cry it out. Yell it out and be angry. But instead of choosing an avenue of virtue signaling, i.e. posting hashtags and calling it a day, process your emotions with other white people you know who have been doing the work for a while—the work in dismantling systemic racism. Read the books and process with these friends. There really *is* such a thing as white guilt. When we place our white guilt on our Friends of Color, we are compounding the pain many have felt for their whole lives along with the most recent tragedy of watching an innocent Black man, woman, or child die needlessly from police brutality and then never see justice.

Examine Your Own Bias

Read the books. Watch the Netflix series. Allow your heart to be broken. Allow the scales to fall from your eyes. And when you feel broken, fill yourself up with actionable steps you can do every day: **listen** to your Friends of Color, examine your bias and fears that you have when you encounter disciplining your Students of Color or when you talk with their parents, listen to TED Talks, and truly reflect on exactly what your role has been in silencing others or where you have been wrong. Pledge and contribute to organizations designed to empower People of Color, such as the NAACP, join peaceful protests, and support Black-owned businesses. This kind of work won't always be picture perfect for social media, and it isn't an easy fix if you have been silent about racism for years. But it is the beginning, and it's the first place you should start, or nothing else really matters regarding your role in making changes to dismantle a society built on systemic racism. Google "systemic racism" if you aren't sure what it is or means.

Talk with your children. Your children are probably very aware of what is going on if you have had the news on or if they have attended public school. They probably have heard the N-word and maybe have even used it. Ask for their thoughts and start the conversation. A great place to start with children is to read and learn about the many People of Color who have helped our nation develop in innovation, medicine, the arts, and business. Starting the journey of becoming anti-racist starts in ourselves and our homes.

Taking Action

It's challenging to know when to speak out and when to stay silent, and both are necessary actions when showing solidarity to our friends. Sometimes our Friends of Color need us to use our white platforms to speak out. But other times, when they are speaking, we can use our platforms to amplify theirs. How will you know when to do either? When it's not about you. There's the pain of guilt you first feel when you finally see the discrimination our friends have dealt with for years. But that is different from the pain you feel when you see an innocent man or woman's life snuffed out, knowing their family has a lifetime of grief to follow. One source of pain is about you, and the other is about someone you probably don't know whose life was ended by murder. When you choose your words, if you do use your words, make it about them.

Embrace the awkward and uncomfortable feeling that you are doing this all wrong. If you are just beginning this journey, you probably are going about it all wrong. If you stop, it was all superficial, but if you continue to learn and do better, the proof of your commitment will show. You aren't above a sincere apology when needed. You probably will have to be called in for saying or doing something insensitive. Your willingness to be humbled in this process is proof of your commitment.

This is not a feel-good journey. It's painful and grievous. The ignorant bliss that kept you from seeing racial trauma is no more. Once you begin this journey, you will start looking at each of your life's decisions through a lens of privilege afforded to you because you are the "right" color by White society's standards. This doesn't mean you won't experience joy in this mission, but knowing the joy of your work will cost you.

The Cost

The cost will be friends and family who feel unburdened to put you in your place without any respect. Some will accuse you of being offensive, call you a name, or label you unfairly. You may lose followers or people who you thought were your friends. The truth is that you cannot make the choice of learning to be anti-racist for them. The people who choose not to do this work are making a choice to stay ignorant in the face of the undeniable truth of the injustice that People of Color have endured for hundreds of years. Your commitment will show when you keep going and keep learning despite their actions against you.

People who want to stay comfortable will often say that talking about race in America divides us, not the racist institutions that we finally see for ourselves. That is a myth. If you can talk about it with others in a respectful way, you are doing something we've largely ignored for the last four hundred years. If we can't talk about it, we can't learn from each other. When your Friend of Color tells you about their life's journey and discrimination as part of it, believe them. Don't silence them by saying it can't be true. It is true. Again, believe them. Let their words soak into your heart and mind and drive you to make changes in your unique circle of influence.

This change in your lifestyle, of being intentional to be anti-racist, will feel very awkward and then even exhausting. As a white person, it is our privilege to have just begun or even enter this arena for the first time. We entered late. The fact that we are just now showing up is still very hurtful for our Black, Indigenous, and People of Color (BIPOC) friends. So the commitment we make needs to be filled with humility and knowledge that we could ignore their reality for too long. But don't let that stop you. Talk with your supervisor about hiring more BIPOC. Support your local or state chapter of the National Alliance of Black School Educators (NABSE). Don't be afraid to be the only white person in a setting. All of the discomfort you feel actually grows you in the process of becoming anti-racist.

Using Your Platform for Change

Our platform isn't for the haters. People will find reasons to cancel or hate us. People will try and shut you down for speaking out or advocating in protest. Our platform is for those who listen and learn from us. That's why our silence is so deafening. When we refuse to acknowledge racism or racist behavior, those who learn from us think that is how to approach it. If we want our children or students to grow up knowing better, they must see us taking action first.

Whether you have been doing the work for equity in education and life for a long time, or you have just started, there truly is power in our voices when we come together. If you can help guide another, help them. It can be frustrating that others are just now-finally-seeing injustice, but nothing good comes from self-righteousness. Keeping others' dignity intact, though it may seem hard, helps them to continue their commitment to see and end racism.

Lastly, we always have a choice. When we begin the work and

commit to it, staying silent is no longer one of them. On this journey, we will be too much for some to hear and not enough for others. We will do and say too much so others will tune us out. Others will claim we are lukewarm and still not doing enough. It's just how it goes. But remember, why did we embark on this journey? For praise or for change? If it's for change, don't stop. Don't ever stop.

Melody McAllister

Melody McAllister is a wife, mother of five, educator, and author. She and her family relocated to Alaska from the Dallas area in 2019. McAllister is 2017 Garland, TX NAACP Educator of the Year and author of the I'm Sorry Story, a children's book about taking responsibility for mistakes and making sincere apologies. She loves to share her story with children all over the world and has done many virtual author read alouds in the United States, Germany, and Uganda! She is also the Logistics Manager for EduMatch Publishing and consults with other educators who are looking to enhance their social media presence. McAllister has spoken at ISTE and ASTE and in different educational panels about equity issues in education, and writes about her journey in her blog, HeGaveMeAMelody.com. She loves the writing community and regularly features authors and educators on her Facebook page, Facebook.com/mjmcalliwrites. Follow her on Twitter and Instagram @mjmcalliwrites.

10

BELONGING BEFORE BLOOM, NOT MASLOW BEFORE BLOOM

DR. ILENE WINOKUR

Introduction

The phrase "Maslow Before Bloom" has become very popular these days in light of the increased focus on social and emotional learning (SEL) and trauma-informed pedagogy. Educators believe that focusing on Maslow's hierarchy means children's need to feel safe and secure will set them up for success in their learning. However, while educators might know about Abraham Maslow's hierarchy of needs, they might not be aware that Maslow's pyramid was deeply influenced by the teachings of the Blackfoot Confederation after he spent time with them during the summer of 1938. According to Edward Hoffman, the author of his biography, Maslow had high respect for their beliefs. I found this out recently after seeing a post on Twitter showing a graphic of the pyramid on one side and the Blackfoot tipi on the other. I was curious to know more, so I began research on Maslow's theory. I discovered that he didn't gather research other than case studies from his practice and motivational psychology expertise. This made me even more curious, so I continued to search online and found a blog post by Barbara Bray and recalled that she had also written about it in her latest book, *Define Your Why* (Bray, 2020, pp. 161-163). Bray explains she read an interview with Dr. Cindy Blackstock, who describes Maslow's connection to the Blackfoot Nation. As Bray explains, "(s)elf-actualization is at the base of the tipi, not at the top, and is the foundation on which community actualization is built" (p. 162). The Blackfoot's tipi refers to "cultural perpetuity" as a human's ultimate goal. Broadly interpreted, cultural perpetuity is leaving behind a legacy that others in the community can emulate, thus perpetuating the good in society.

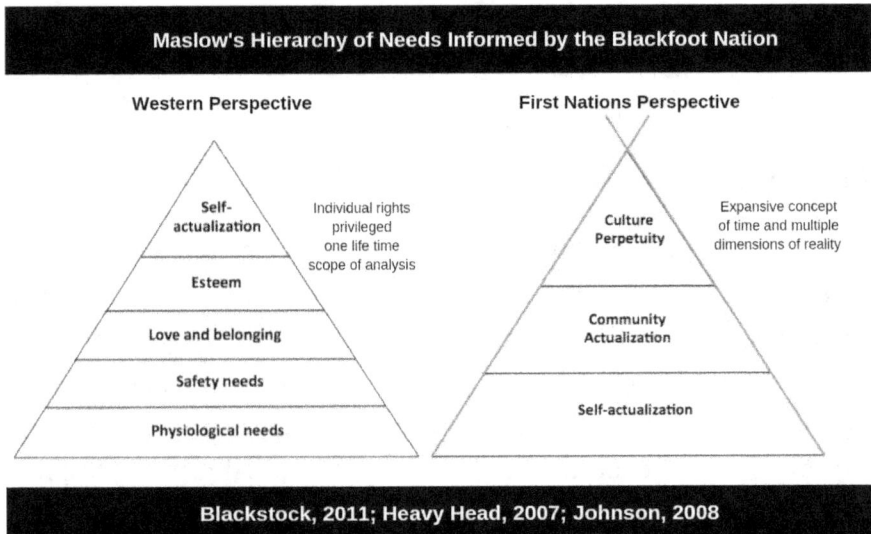

Source: Bray, B. (2020). *Define Your Why: Own your story so you can live and learn on purpose*. EduMatch®.

Maslow's hierarchy of needs focuses on individual motivation, rather than community, and includes a sequence of stages; until you fulfill a stage, you cannot move to the next one. Maslow's first stage is physiological (food, clothing, and shelter). He believed that once physiological needs are met, safety is next (personal security, health, employment). After physiological and safety are met, love and belonging (connection, friendship, family) can be achieved. Esteem (respect, status, recognition) is the next rung up, and, finally, self-actualization (to become the best we can be). He believed that the path to self-actualization (the ultimate goal we want to reach) is linear, meaning if we miss a step, we cannot move to the next. However, belonging isn't linear. It happens at every stage of our lives. We encounter the need to belong all our lives. Esteem creates one of the conditions for belonging. Once we feel valued and respected, we can feel safe and that we belong because we are accepted for our authentic selves.

My journey to understand my life in two different cultures on different sides of the world led me to read about belonging to understand what makes it essential for us to thrive and succeed. I read that to feel a sense of belonging, we need to feel safe, to feel that we can be our authentic selves, not pretending to "fit in" with others by being the same as them. After learning more about belonging, I concluded that Maslow got it wrong. So what do I believe Maslow got wrong? Rather than a hierarchy, the steps intertwine and go back and forth, in and out. They change as we experience different stages of our lives. Safety and belonging are the prerequisite conditions for happiness, satisfaction, success, and achievement. But we can be our best selves as we move back and forth between the stages and experiences. Part of feeling safe is having basic needs met, such as food, clothing, and a roof over our heads. These don't happen in a step by step manner. Feeling a sense of belonging is a continuum that we move back and forth throughout our lives. The focus should be on belonging and creating a safe space to ensure each of us finds that sense of belonging. I concluded, after reading the psychology, physiology, and education literature, there are three types of belonging: Self, Personal, and Professional. Ultimately, our goal should be to become a good ancestor, to be remembered, and to serve as a model for others to follow.

In education, students need to feel safe and a sense of belonging before they can concentrate on their learning. For that reason, I believe in Belonging before Bloom, not Maslow before Bloom. Maslow believed people are motivated to reach self-actualization, but that shouldn't be our ultimate goal in life. It's where we need to start. The first three tiers of Maslow's hierarchy are all part of feeling safe and self-confident, which is essential to belonging and the basis for wellbeing. Those tiers should be combined because you can't have one without the other. There isn't a step by step hierarchy to fulfilling physiological needs, then safety needs, and then belonging and love. Finding our sense of belonging changes and grows throughout our lives.

Maslow believed that people were motivated once they reached self-actualization. He turned the Blackfoot tipi upside down and left self-actualization as our ultimate goal. In his interpretation, the realization of one's potential is a motivating force towards self-actualization: *the realization or fulfillment of one's talents and potentialities, especially considered as a drive or need present in everyone.* Simply stated, for each individual to be self-actualized, we must first meet all the other criteria of his pyramid of needs. Otherwise, we are unable to achieve self-fulfillment. Maslow's focus is on individual motivations, a Western perception of human development. However, he missed a major point. Humans need to feel connected; they need to feel a sense of community and belonging, so if our ultimate goal is individual, how will that make us feel fulfilled? I argue that it doesn't. Our ultimate goal as humans is to become good ancestors and leave a legacy once we are gone that reminds those left behind about the way life should be lived.

I will share some vignettes from my life that demonstrate the three types of belonging and our goal to leave a legacy that sets an example for others to follow. My personal story is filled with connections to belonging. As I read through the various articles and studies about belonging, I put my own experiences into each context. I realized that my motivation for self-actualization or feeling valued, appreciated for my true self, and genuinely recognized by others was necessary before I could have healthy personal and professional relationships with others. It wasn't until I gained self-confidence, self-efficacy, and self-worth that I began to experience feelings of belonging within my communities.

The steps to achieve success and happiness in our lives are self-belonging, personal belonging, and professional belonging. Once we have achieved all three, we can become a good ancestor.

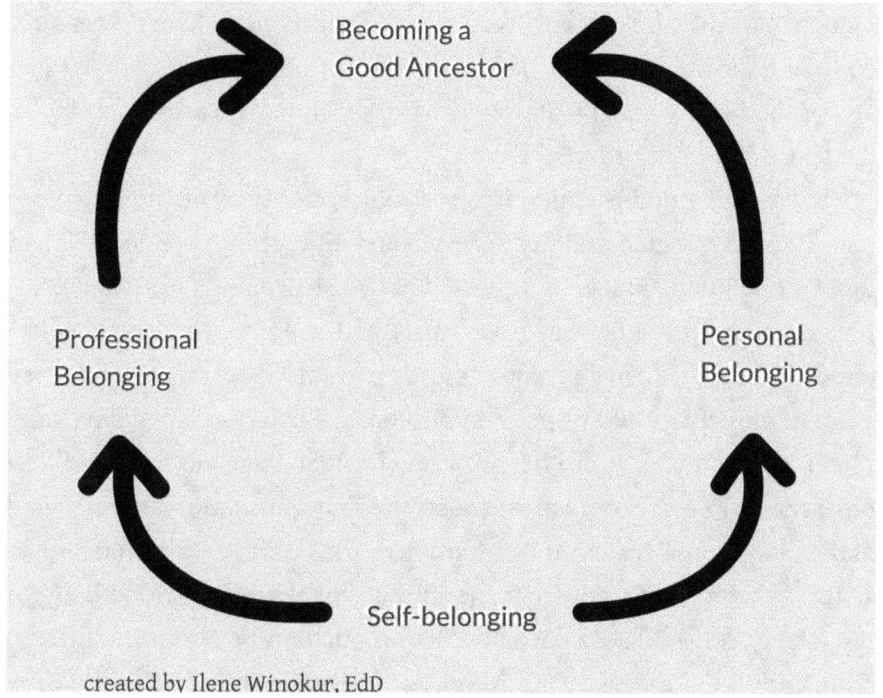

created by Ilene Winokur, EdD

Self-Belonging (self-awareness, self-confidence, self-efficacy)

Once we feel a sense of belonging, we gain self-confidence, realize our self-worth, and can spend time alone without feeling lonely.

My sense of belonging began in Buffalo, New York, where I grew up. My mother was a "stay at home" mom until I was 12, and she began her undergraduate studies at a local university. She cooked, baked, cleaned, and took care of me, my older brother, and little sister. I was born on Long Island, New York but moved with my family in 1962 at the age of 6 years to Buffalo, NY, where my father had been promoted and transferred by the New York State Department of Labor. I had finished kindergarten and started first grade in a new school that happened to be located directly across the street from our house. I loved walking to school since I had taken the bus at my previous school. We had a big backyard, and our house was much bigger than the house we moved from. The biggest change was very cold and snowy winters. I had to be careful not to get frostbite, so I always had shiny cheeks plastered with Vaseline. It was fun to play in the snow, but I didn't like the cold.

I was the middle child of three siblings. My brother was more than five years older, and my sister, nearly five years younger. We had family dinners at 5:30 p.m. every day. Most evenings, the conversation revolved around what each of us had accomplished or encountered that day. When my parents didn't want us to know what they were talking about, they spoke in broken Yiddish (the language of my father's parents). My brother was much older than me, so we didn't have much in common. He was also involved in school activities and active as a youth leader at our temple, so I didn't see him much. My sister was very different from me in many ways and also the baby of the family, so she had a special place in our family. She also suffered from childhood illnesses and weight problems even in her early years, which occupied my mother a lot of the time. Being a middle child made me very quiet.

School was also stressful for me. Although I was a good student, by the time I entered grade 7, which was junior high school at the time (middle school now), I had been in five different school buildings with different classmates each time. I had so much anxiety about meeting new people, getting adjusted to new school surroundings, and getting through the year that it left me quite upended. Third grade was my first year living in a new neighborhood and a mixed year for me. Since I was shy and quiet, I had trouble making friends. However, I had a wonderful teacher who made me feel welcome and special. She sent notes home to my parents, telling them how helpful and patient I was. Unfortunately, this school was the only kindergarten through grade 3, which meant I had to move to another building for grade 4. I don't remember much of the two years I spent at that school except that I played the role of Mary Poppins and carried an umbrella as my prop. I attended sixth grade in another building, which was in the opposite direction of my two previous schools. Each time I moved, I lost contact with the few friends I had made. It was almost impossible for me to find any attachment to other classmates when I knew I would be moving to another school building within a short time.

Then I moved to the junior high (now known as middle school). I was finally able to spend three years in the same building. My seventh grade English teacher, Miss Fox, was an innovator and one of the teachers I still remember after 50 years. She let us get to know her personally by sharing her travel adventures with us. She had visited Japan the summer before she taught us and brought dried seaweed into class for us to try. Our poetry unit included song lyrics by the Beatles and Simon and Garfunkle. She and I were kindred spirits! I had finally found a teacher who understood me and made me feel safe. It was an awesome year, and I blossomed. I tried out for the school play and became friends with several students. I finally believed in myself and gained the confidence to try new things.

Being alone without feeling lonely is the ultimate goal for self-belonging.

Personal Belonging (relationships with family and friends; teacher and student; co-regulation among people you know and trust)

Having a sense of personal belonging supports healthy relationships and our ability to cope with stress and trauma.

In 1984, I moved to Kuwait after meeting my soulmate, a graduate student. We were married in Kuwait, and I immediately became part of my husband's family and circle of friends. My brother-in-law and his wife were the first to invite us to their weekend "chalet." It was a lovely day in late November and still warm enough to go swimming. My sister-in-law didn't speak English, so we had a younger cousin of hers translate as we walked along the beach. She asked me many questions about my interests and offered a lot of advice about living a good life in Kuwait. I appreciated how much she cared about me even though she hardly knew me! Later, I found out that my husband was very special to her and my brother-in-law, so they wanted to make sure I was happy and comfortable in Kuwait. Other relatives made similar efforts to ensure I was comfortable and happy in my new home and felt I belonged.

Another way I felt I belonged was my mother-in-law's consistent invitations to join her whenever family and friends visited. If I was upstairs in our apartment, she would call me to let me know someone had arrived for a visit. I would trot downstairs and listen intently to all the foreign sounds and then share the tea and sweets that were offered. I learned how to offer tea to visitors and help with sharing sweets and savories that were set out for all to enjoy.

During the first few years, I didn't understand much of the conversations conducted in Arabic by the older visitors. Still, I listened carefully and asked about words I heard repeated. Some visitors spoke English and made an extra effort to include me in the conversation. Little by little, I learned basic vocabulary and was able to have simple conversations. This was highly appreciated by all since they loved hearing me try out my Arabic. Eventually, I began to put all of it together and was able to have short conversations about popular subjects. With practice and a lot of listening, I was finally able to have extended conversations. One day during a family gathering, my brother-in-law asked me how I could understand his wife. I replied that I was able to understand simple conversations. He interrupted me and said, "No, I mean, how do you understand her? She uses so many old Kuwaiti words that we don't use anymore and that I don't even know." I thought for a minute or two and then realized the reason. I spent every free moment with my mother-in-law and her older relatives and friends, which exposed me to their vocabulary. I never know what those words or phrases are until someone I am talking with giggles. Then I know I've said something they didn't expect me to know.

All of this made me feel "at home" in Kuwait. I felt valued and accepted. I felt I "belonged." My sisters-in-law took me shopping and invited me to visit their extended families. When my children were sick, they gave me advice about doctors and medicine, especially old home remedies. I have been very lucky, and I have also made an effort to learn the language and culture of Kuwait. I studied its history and learned to appreciate how far they have come in a relatively short time.

Once we establish healthy relationships with family and friends, we can overcome stressful situations and push through traumatic experiences.

Professional Belonging (building our PLN community; collegiality at work; co-regulation among people you work with and trust)

Professional belonging depends on the quality of our relationships at work.

In 2016, when I was still mostly a lurker on Twitter, I came across a post by someone in my PLN (honestly, I would give credit here, but I don't remember who posted the information) who was #notatISTE and posted links to live streaming of some sessions at the conference. As I watched, I felt this strong connection to those attending. I also found #passthescopeEDU was interviewing attendees, which gave me an inside look at all the activities that happen during the conference. I was hooked! and made up my mind that I would join right away and attend the 2017 conference in El Paso, Texas. Looking back, I realize that it was a life-changing moment that opened up my world to edtech, amazing people to add to my PLN, and moved me out of my comfort zone.

People don't usually move out of their comfort zones unless they feel welcome, included, and accepted. Finding a sense of self-belonging within ISTE meant I had to gain confidence and feel accepted for my lack of knowledge about edtech but a willingness to learn. I found all of that and more among the ISTE community. Alison Taplay, in a comment on a blog post from October 2018, writes, "(Belonging) is a feeling of connection to others and a connection to place. It means feeling welcomed and accepted. It means feeling safe enough to be me; to show up and contribute! When everyone in a community experiences this sense of belonging, there is a natural shift toward an attitude of taking care of one another."

During the year leading up to the 2017 conference, I began to follow others who were involved in edtech and ISTE PLNs. I made sure I received the regular newsletters and updates from ISTE and my

ISTE PLNs. I added my name to the Global Collaboration Network and indicated my interest in volunteering for the leadership team; I became an at large member and loved attending the synchronous meetings and supporting the planning of conference activities like the Playground and Scavenger Hunt. I got to know the rest of the team and learned so much from them. Also, I added my name to the ISTE17 group and learned how to make the most out of the conference (it's packed with so many things going on at once that it's easy to get overwhelmed and FOMO if you're not careful). All of this made me feel valued. Everyone needs to feel valued.

In June 2017, I attended the conference in El Paso. ISTE17 was daunting, but I was determined to meet people and make the most of my five-day experience. The Badge Summit was my first day. I have always been interested in digital badges as a way to show competency mastery for personal and professional development. I had no idea that I would meet someone I had been following for a while and admired for her knowledge and caring about education and educators. That special person is Barbara Bray. Barbara saw me sitting alone at one of the Badge Summit sessions, and, as she told me later, she dislikes seeing anyone sit alone. She joined me at my table, and we struck up a conversation. If you know Barbara, you know that it's immensely difficult to resist chatting with her. She is one of the nicest and friendliest people you will ever meet and so good at networking! After the session finished, she asked if I'd like to join her to attend a special event later that evening. I was thrilled and felt so honored. Here was someone I considered an education icon asking me to join her. I'm quite shy and introverted, so my answer normally would have been, "That's nice, but I think I'll just go back to the hotel." However, there was something about Barbara that made me feel like we had known each other forever. It was the beginning of our friendship and sisterhood. We've been roommates at ISTE since then and keep in touch often even though she's in California and I'm in Kuwait.

There is something else about Barbara that I want to mention here. She opened doors for me to go through that I never would have had the courage to enter. She connected me with other amazing and caring educators who helped me grow over the past three years. When you're at ISTE, there are thousands of people around you, but if you recognize someone you've been following on social media, time slows down, and as you bound across the room to hug that person, they welcome you and make you feel special too. Besides the amazing networking opportunities at ISTE, there are a variety of sessions and special events like Flipgrid Live and EdTech Karaoke. But probably my favorite is the GCN Scavenger Hunt. Barbara and I teamed up with three other amazing women, Heidi Carr, Melissa Eddington, and Christy Cate. Even my children were surprised at the things I was willing to do, like making a pyramid with the rest of my team (like cheerleaders do) or asking a stranger who sort of looked like me to pose for a photo (in the middle of Chicago's Chinatown). I don't think I've ever had that much fun!

ISTE members welcomed me with open arms and created the opportunity to meet so many awesome people who have made such a difference in my life. Because I feel like I have people I can count on for support at any time, I continue to venture out of my comfort zone. I'm more active on social media and speak out about causes I believe in. I am also learning how to use apps and showing others how to use them. At ISTE, Sharing definitely does mean Caring! A membership in ISTE is a gift that keeps on giving.

We can risk failure and have a growth mindset in our professional life when our feeling of professional belonging is strong.

Becoming a Good Ancestor: Our Legacy (serving as a positive model or influence to others)

We often hear about famous people who have impacted the lives of others and left a legacy as an example for others to follow. I have also begun hearing about being a "good ancestor," which equates to leaving a legacy of kindness, equity, inclusivity, and embracing diversity. This is something we should all strive for, being remembered for the good work we did and that we are an example for others to follow. Authors and educators Layla F. Saad and Bina Venkataraman believe that our future relies on cultural perpetuity, as the Blackfoot believed. Saad's book, *Me and White Supremacy* (2020), is a step by step guide for anti-racism. Those who do the hard work of unpacking their biases can become advocates for equity, diversity, and inclusion. In *The Optimist's Telescope* (2019), Venkataraman discusses the difficulty we have thinking about the future when making present-day decisions.

The first good ancestor in my life was my father. He died in 2009 at the age of 88. He was gone in a minute, but he still lives in the hearts and minds of many. You might wonder why he was so special that people still recall his positive impact on their lives. One word: belonging.

My father, Douglas Louis Winokur (some knew him as Doug, others as Lou), grew up in a family of immigrant parents. His mother never learned English; she only spoke Yiddish. His father was a furrier, a skilled craftsman who started a family business after arriving in the United States. My father was the second youngest of five. He was a good student and highly thought of by peers and teachers. While he was in law school, World War II began. He left school, enlisted in the army, and was assigned to help out in a medic unit of the army. He served in France, where his skill with the French language he'd learned in high school and Yiddish, which he spoke at home and is close to German, made him an ideal translator for injured German prisoners brought to the field hospital.

When he returned to America, he completed law school, married my mother, and took a government job working in the psychiatric ward of a hospital. He never spoke to us much about the few years he worked there but offered advice related to his experiences when it was appropriate. I always felt it was a difficult time for him. One of the perks of working for the New York State State government is the ability to take civil service tests, which, when passed, moves you up the ranks and opens up different job opportunities. Eventually, my father qualified for a job in the New York State Employment Service. He slowly moved his way up the ladder and was eventually promoted to assistant superintendent in the Western New York area. So in 1962, we moved to Buffalo. All the while, he was an inclusive leader who made sure those he worked with felt valued and accepted.

Throughout his life, my father stood up for those who were treated unfairly in their job. He also accepted differences and made sure his children, my brother, sister, and I followed the same. During the Civil Rights movement, he spoke out about equal pay and equal job opportunities based on qualifications and not on race, religion, or ethnicity. He was indeed upholding the law, but he was doing it at a time of transition when many disagreed with him, and some employers tried to keep things as they were before the U.S. Constitutional Amendment passed in 1964. My father stood his ground and continued to support equal rights for jobs and salaries and equitable treatment throughout his career. All this time, he brought his beliefs into our home and our neighborhood. He was never silent.

After he retired, he volunteered as a lawyer to support those who couldn't afford legal representation, and later on, opened a private law office with several other lawyers. He represented and counseled clients to help them out of financial problems and advised them about real estate transactions. All the while, he continued to uphold his belief in equal opportunity. His clients knew they could trust him to represent them in a way that looked out for their best interests, even though sometimes they didn't agree with him.

After he died, many of his former employees, clients, and neighbors recalled his contribution to making their lives better. My family knew he was pretty amazing, but we had no idea how much of an impact he'd had on others over the years.

This is Douglas L. Winokur's legacy. He left his children and grandchildren with a solid foundation of love, caring, and acceptance, the basics of belonging. He was an example to everyone he met throughout his life, and he is remembered for his good efforts and work to make this world a better place. He is truly a good ancestor.

Becoming a good ancestor is the ultimate goal in our lives. Once we feel a sense of belonging and acceptance for our authentic selves, we pass on what we've learned so others can learn and grow from our legacy.

Epilogue

Our students come to our classrooms with personal stories that are sometimes quite overwhelming. Our responsibility as teachers is to uncover the reasons behind their behaviors that may appear disruptive. Social and emotional learning (SEL) and trauma-informed teaching are vital for us to ensure that all students learn, and that begins by helping them feel a sense of belonging within a safe space. They need to believe in their own self-worth before they can make a personal connection with their teacher and be on a path to wellbeing and learning. Belonging before Bloom.

References

Bray, B. (2020). *Define your why: Own your story so you can live and learn on purpose.* EduMatch®.

Hoffman, E. (1988). *The right to be human: A biography of Abraham Maslow.* Jeremy P. Tarcher, Inc.

Saad, L. F. (2020). *Me and white supremacy: Combat Racism, change the world, and become a good ancestor.* Sourcebooks.

Taplay, A. (2018, October 18). *What does belonging mean to you?* WordPress. https://wordpress.viu.ca/belonging/2018/10/12/hello-world

Venkataraman, B. (2019). *The optimist's telescope: Thinking ahead in a reckless age.* Riverhead Books.

Belonging Before Bloom, Not Maslow Before Bloom

Dr. Ilene Winokur

Dr. Ilene Winokur AlZaid has lived in Kuwait for over 35 years and retired in June 2019 as Director of the Foundation Program Unit (Math and English) at Gulf University for Science and Technology (GUST). She also founded and managed a professional development consultancy in Kuwait. She taught and was an administrator at the early childhood and elementary levels, in addition to teaching and administration at the college level in private institutions in Kuwait for 20 years. Her academic interests are leadership in practice, social emotional learning, blended learning, and continuing professional development (CPD).

Ilene served on the steering committee for accreditation, co-wrote and edited the content-area curriculum, and later supervised the revision of the curriculum using a "backward design" at a local private American school in Kuwait. During her tenure as elementary principal, she supervised a revision of the elementary school report card based on the level of skills students achieved. She has presented workshops at local and regional conferences and local school professional development days on topics including Kuwaiti culture, the administrator as a visionary leader, and Bloom's taxonomy. She has also mentored struggling teachers and aspiring administrators. As an administrator, she encouraged members of her staff to become teacher leaders.

Ilene earned a doctorate in Educational Leadership from Lehigh University and an MBA from the University of Miami, Florida. She also completed ESL certification from the College of New Jersey, and a BA in History from State University at Buffalo, New York. Ilene has over 20 years of experience in teaching, mentoring and administration.

Ilene currently volunteers and supports refugee teachers and students. She is very active on Twitter @IleneWinokur where she grows her PLN. She is also a Community Leader for Wakelet and a Buncee Ambassador. She believes in the power of global connections and collaboration which she supports by being an active member of ISTE's Global Collaboration PLN and TESOL Refugee Concerns Interest Section Member at Large. You can find her blog, podcast and more information about her on her website: https://journeys2belonging.webstarts.com

11

TALKING ABOUT SUICIDE WITH CHILDREN

DR. DEBORAH KERBY, ED. D.

Suicide is a leading cause of death, and the topic should be open for discussion. When we bring problems into the light, they often don't seem as scary.

Why We Should Talk About Suicide

First, let me say that I am not a counselor or formally trained in psychology. My thoughts and opinions on this subject are based on 20 years as a classroom teacher and a lifetime raising children. That said, it is surprising to me that at this time, though suicide is a leading cause of death (Gibbons, Hur, Lavigne, Wange, and Mann, 2019), it is not included as a topic of discussion in health classes for junior high and high school students. According to the National Institute of Mental Health (2019), "Suicide was the second leading cause of death among individuals between the ages of 10 and 34" (p. 1). There were more suicides among children aged 10 to 24 than deaths from homicide, cancer, or other diseases.

Health curriculums are full of graphic details on sexually transmitted diseases (STDs), which most of our students will never contract. According to the Center for Disease Control and Prevention (2020), only 40 percent of U.S. teens "have ever had sexual intercourse" (p. 1), and less than half of them will catch an STD. Yet, suicide, which will impact at least 25 percent of our students (Pompili, Shrivastava, Serafini, et al., 2020), is not discussed. Perhaps some of the time allocated for public school health classes to discuss STDs could be made available for talking about mental health issues, communication skills, and suicide.

About eight years ago, I discovered how interested my students were on this topic. It came up in the class during one of those teachable moments. I don't remember the specifics; I do remember that every head in the room snapped to attention. People want to talk about suicide, but it is understood to be a "taboo" topic; there is a "stigma associated with asking for help" (Suicide Prevention Lifeline (n.d.). , p.1). Some hesitate to discuss the topic because they fear talking about suicide will plant the idea in one's mind, but the opposite may be true (Rudlin, 2020). Demonstrating a willingness to discuss the topic may lead a child to seek help.

What We Should Be Aware Of

Some students will talk about suicide because they are trying to get sympathy or attention. But, even if you think this is the case, do not disregard the situation. Many young people talk about death or hating life before they attempt suicide. So, even if you think an attempt is unlikely, it is important to take it seriously. One may be trying to get attention by talking about it today, but tomorrow they may take more serious measures to get attention. If someone is talking about suicide, s/he is thinking about harming themself to some degree.

There are many triggers for suicidal thoughts. Change of relationship status is a big one. Also, take note if you know a child has existing mental health issues, an inadequate support system, or recent experience with a loved one who died from suicide. Some other potential areas of concern are drug or alcohol use, bullying or abuse, or some other major change in one's life, including changes to gender or sexual identification (Healthy Children.org, 2017; Suicide Prevention Lifeline, n.d.). It is also common for someone to exhibit a drastic change in behavior when they have decided to end their life. For instance, someone who is normally very messy may clean up their room; someone who is normally neat may start leaving big messes.

Antidepressants and other medications have been known to increase the risk of suicide, particularly in young people (Mauney, 2020). "Antidepressants could double the likelihood of a patient becoming suicidal if that person was not truly clinically depressed before taking the medications" (p. 2). Gibbons, Kwan Hur, Lavigne, Wange, and Mann (2019) found ten medications that may increase the risk of suicide, including alprazolam, cyclobenzaprine, the commonly prescribed steroid prednisone, and the antibiotic azithromycin.

What To Tell Students

It is no wonder junior high and high school students get depressed. They are going through physical changes; some are disturbing, some embarrassing. Their hormones are all over the place. Many deal with bullying from teachers and peers. Many are frustrated, feeling like they are grown up and able to make decisions but want to be held and comforted. English class literature consists primarily of tragedies. In recent years, young people have the added pressure of having to choose not only a sexuality but a gender. And on top of all this, adults are telling them this is the best time of their life!

A very important point to stress is that suicide is a permanent solution to a temporary problem. Everything is temporary. If you think this is the worst time of your life, it very well may be, but it will come to an end. Let them know that though you might not have an answer for them now but that you are willing to explore ideas together. Young people need to know they are not alone. If possible, make sure they are not left on their own when they leave school (Rudlin, 2020). You might suggest they join a club or participate in activities open to young people in the neighborhood.

Tell your students that this is NOT the best time of their life; it gets better. Many of us start to really understand who we are and what we want in our 30s. By our 40s, we, hopefully, are in a place where we are not struggling financially and can live the lifestyle that suits us. Most people in their 50s have gotten to a place where it doesn't matter what other people say anymore, which gives them confidence. I cannot tell you about the 60s or beyond yet; I just know that it keeps getting better. Share this with students. I wish someone had shared it with me when I was a teenager. Many who attempt suicide choose that path because they feel that their life will never get better. Letting them know it will get better may give them the shred of hope they need.

Suggest that your students get more fresh air and exercise, and also that they do volunteer work. One of the best ways to feel better about one's life is to spend time doing for others.

Resources

National Suicide Prevention Lifeline

- Phone 1-800-273-8255
- Youth resources page https://suicidepreventionlifeline.org/help-yourself/youth/
- Loss survivors https://suicidepreventionlifeline.org/help-yourself/loss-survivors/

- Find a grief counselor https://www.sosmadison.com/resources/clinical-support
- Find a suicidal ideation therapist https://www.psychologytoday.com/us/therapists/suicidal-ideation

References

Center for Disease Control and Prevention. (2020, March 25). Sexual Risk Behaviors Can Lead to HIV, STDS, & Teen Pregnancy. https://www.cdc.gov/healthyyouth/sexualbehaviors/index.htm

Gibbons, R., Hur, K., Lavigne, J., Wang, J., & Mann, J. J. (2019). Medications and suicide: High dimensional empirical bayes screening (iDEAS). Harvard Data Science Review, 1(2). https://doi.org/10.1162/99608f92.6fdaa9de

Mauney, M. (2020, August 19). Suicide and antidepressants. Drugwatch.com. https://www.drugwatch.com/ssri/suicide

National Institute of Mental Health (NIMH). (2020, April). Suicide. https://www.nimh.nih.gov/health/statistics/suicide.shtml

Pompili, M., Shrivastava, A., Serafini, G., Innamorati, M., Milelli, M., Erbuto, D., Ricci,

F., Lamis, D. A., Scocco, P., Amore, M., Lester, D., & Girardi, P. (2013). Bereavement after the suicide of a significant other. Indian journal of psychiatry, 55(3), 256–263. https://doi.org/10.4103/0019-5545.117145

Rudlin, K. (2020). What to say to a suicidal teen. https://www.verywellmind.com/what-to-say-to-a-suicidal-teen-2611331

Suicide Prevention Lifeline (n.d.). We can all prevent suicide. https://suicidepreventionlifeline.org/how-we-can-all-prevent-suicide/

Deborah Kerby teaches K-6 Computer Skills and Computer Science at a public school in Northeast, PA. Before teaching elementary she taught 16 years of Business and Computer classes at Pocono Mountain East High School. Deborah earned a Doctorate in Education Leadership, as well as a Certificate in Instructional Technology, from Wilkes University. Before a career in teaching she worked in Business doing Computer and Networking Support, Database Design, Programming and Accounting. She has presented on Adaptive Learning with Google Forms in a Webinar and a face-to-face session through ISTE. She also regularly contacts legislators in Harrisburg, PA and Washington, D.C. about improving education. She also regularly contacts legislators in Harrisburg, PA and Washington, D.C. about improving education.

12

THERE ARE NO BAD KIDS

AUBREY JONES

Behavior as communication

As I watched Jonah watch the epic scene from *Toy Story* for the fifth time, I wondered what he was seeing, learning, or trying to tell me. It was the same scene, and he was distressed. His mom was frustrated and scared. She was at her wit's end. Exhausted and worn out. She had just celebrated her 40th birthday. Her son was shuttled back and forth from doctors, appointments, and school.

He was labeled as aggressive, bad. He was a bad kid, according to teachers and medical professionals. Each day, his mom became more and more burdened with his behavior and less alleviated with answers. As I watched the scene from *Toy Story* play again on his screen, I could not help but think, "What is he trying to tell me?"

In the typically developing human world, more than half of communication is non-verbal. We use gestures, facial expressions, and body language to ensure that our message is received. So what was Jonah, who did not have words trying to tell us through this scene of *Toy Story?*

As the scene played for a third time on the screen, I couldn't help but notice that he was getting more frustrated. He was rocking back and forth. Jonah, at 19, could only communicate through the scene playing on his screen and the non-verbal communication tools that he had. He did not have the language to explain what was going on. He became more agitated as the scene repeated for the fourth time. The message was not being received.

I never connected the dots for Jonah to understand that his stomach hurt. He threw up at school the next day and was sent home. Hours later, he was admitted to the emergency room. Jonah had a bowel obstruction. When he played the scene from *Toy Story,* he used his words to tell us he was in pain. When he threw something, he was frustrated that his message was not received.

Jonah is not a bad kid. Jonah is a smart kid who used all the tools that he had to communicate with us. Jonah told us in all the ways that he knew how that he was in pain and needed relief. We (the educated adults in his life) did not receive the message. Unfortunately, we saw all the problems with his behavior instead of the message he was trying to convey.

There are many Jonahs in classrooms that are trying to tell us what is going on with them. If we as educators can flip the lens and see each behavior as a form of communication, we can receive the message that these students are conveying. If we can become detectives to solve these cryptic messages, we will empower our students to communicate with us. Finally, our students will no longer be bad kids, and we can do more to help them achieve in life.

Aubrey Jones

Aubrey wears many hats including special education teacher, behavior analyst and social worker. Simply put, she is Just Aubrey. She looks to eradicate labels in the classroom and in the community. She is on the forefront of a movement entitled #nomorelabels and is working to promote classroom communities of success with structure and support. When she does not have her teacher hat on, she creates comics and loves escaping to the beach. Fueled by caffeine she hopes to push kids (and adults) beyond their comfort zone to try and experience new and exciting things. Really, the bar just needs to be set high enough. She will be opening a resource center (a place for teachers to connect, exchange resources and take care of themselves) in the near future.

Twitter handle: @spedteacheriam
Instagram: @justaubrey87
https://justaubreysthought.blogspot.com

13

NON-VERBALLY COMMUNICATING LOVE

JERRY TOUPS, JR.

Loving your students through non-verbal communication is at the epicenter of a teacher's power of inspiration.

"Mr. Toups
I have loved your class, and I will miss you. Even when I feel down, I come to this class, and I realize that this is like my home. I feel hope in this classroom. I feel like this is the end of the best part of my life. You are an amazing teacher! I will remember everything you taught me, especially the first classroom rule! I will always believe!
Goodbye, sadly
Miranda"

In 1990 when I started my career, I not only inked my first rule as "Always Believe in Yourself," I also made it my goal to be described with words that would impact my kids. Little did I know that these "descriptors" were integrally linked to achieving "teaching" my kids to BELIEVE they can achieve. In the world of public education, we will call these non-verbal actions the "ultimate teacher descriptors."

The "ultimate teacher descriptors" are love, joy, peace, kindness, gentleness, patience, goodness, and faithfulness.

Obviously, I did not make this list up. During my career, I have had students write letters and draw pictures in which these "descriptors" are used. When kids describe who you are with these words, your influence on them becomes dynamic. You will change their lives. You will become a source of hope. You will be a force of goodness to all those around you. This will become evident in the student testimony letters that are found in this writing. **The combination of Always Believe in Yourself as my first rule, and my goal of being described by my students with the ultimate teacher descriptors has been profound. When I started teaching in 1990, I had no idea of the impact this would have on my teachings and classroom management. As a new teacher, I really didn't realize the consequence of these two things on not just the students in my room, but in the school and even the community.** Little did I know back in 1990 when I made my first rule and wanted to be described by my students with the "ultimate teacher descriptors" of the impact that the combination of these two together would be on the literal thousands of kids I have influenced, not just in my classroom, but in the school as a whole. The key to being described with these descriptors is essentially using non-verbal communication. It is one of my life goals as an educator to spread the impact of how both goals will change your students' lives and impact the entirety of your school community.

This skill of using non-verbal communication is evident in the greatest moment of my teaching career. In the spring of 2018, a student came to my room after school and said, "Mr. Toups, I am Carly. I would love to do my senior journalism project as a video documentary about your career."

I was overwhelmed. I did not even teach this child. The video documentary was completed, and in the coworker & student interviews found in the documentary, several of the descriptors are used to describe who I am. The video documentary advanced to the state finals in Austin at the Texas Young Film Makers contest. I was privileged to attend with Carly. Her video "The Story of Always Believe" won 2nd place in her category! While Carly was on the stage being honored, I was beckoned by the crowd to join her. What a magical moment of my career. My influence with my students using these "ultimate teacher descriptors" went beyond the walls of my classroom through the community and eventually to a state audience in an award-winning video documentary: https://youtu.be/lVpqUw1II3k

INSPIRED PHRASE 711 Jerry Toups
Blessings abound when you make your life about others, but when you make your life about the kids in your community, your impact will turn into a legacy.

You are about to learn actions that can be duplicated so your students will describe you with the greatest ultimate teacher descriptor: love. My life is an immensely powerful testimony to this, and my actions can be replicated. When you achieve this, your career will take a different trajectory. You will create a legacy that will persevere after your kids leave your room. You will make a difference.

Before I begin describing the actions of the "ultimate teacher descriptors," let us look at this diagram:

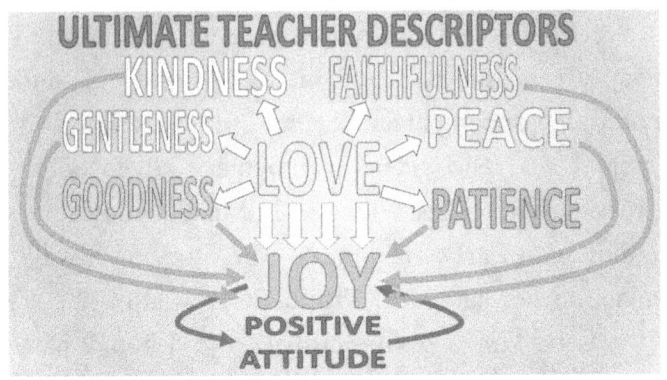

As you can see, LOVE is at the center of these descriptors. Love for the students is the keystone for who you are as an educator. LOVE generates all the other descriptors. All these descriptors together eventually end up generating JOY. This joy will change who you are. Joy is priceless. Joy will be the source of your inspiration to everyone around you. Joy will become a powerful force in a positive attitude cycle that will give your inspiration and non-verbal communication "more power."

Inspired Phrase 935 Jerry Toups
The joy you receive from role modeling the ultimate teacher descriptors is the most powerful source of inspiration you can have over others to promote goodness.

LOVE

Inspired Phrase 41 Jerry Toups
Love someone for who they are and not what you would like them to be.

Non-Verbally Communicating Love

June 3, 2010
Mr. Toups,
Thank you so much for helping me through the past two years. My grandpa died last year, and without even realizing it, you helped me cope with the loss. I did not see a reason to live anymore, but you made me BELIEVE I could survive the depression, and I did. I do not know if I would still be here if it were not for you. You are a wonderful teacher, and you teach more than just math. Thank you sooo much! I will never forget you. You do not know this, but you have been like a father figure to me because my father is never around. I love you for that.
LOVE,
Cheyenne

Every teacher is told to "love" the kids, but no one really tells us how. Verbal communicating your love will only get you so far. Love for your students is primarily generated through non-verbal communication. In the Ultimate Teacher Descriptor diagram, you can see that LOVE is at the heart of inspiration. When you properly love your students through non-verbal communication, the other descriptors can be generated.

Another powerful definition of love is often heard at many weddings. It is in *1st Corinthians 13 4-8 NKJ:*

> *[4] Love is patient and is kind, love does not envy, love does not parade itself, is not puffed up; [5] does not behave rudely, does not seek its own, is not provoked, thinks no evil; [6] does not rejoice in iniquity, but rejoices in truth; [7] bears all things, believes all things, hopes all things, endures all things. [8] Love never fails."*

This definition of love is profound. When you can do these things with your students, your room will become a source of hope. The kids will want to be in your room. You will inspire them. Notice some of the most powerful things in this definition are "nots." Do not envy, do not arrogantly parade your accomplishments, do not be puffed up, do not be rude to the kids, do not seek your own glory. Loving others means you are putting them ahead of you. This is huge. You probably will not survive long in education if you are making your job about "me." Once you realize as a teacher your life is about the kids you have been blessed to influence, it's not about you, but the kids, then your interactions with them will produce love and joy.

While doing Twitter chats, I created this diagram to show how I love my students through non-verbal communication.

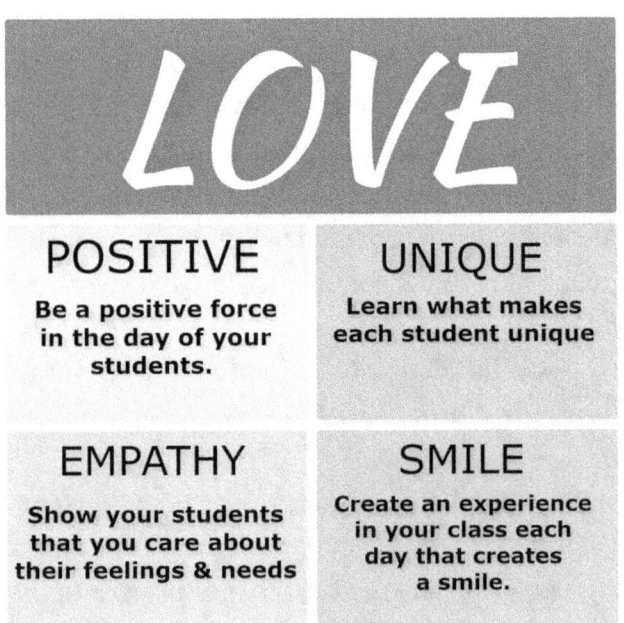

The first step in my diagram to showing your students love is to be a positive force in your students' day. Kids know which teachers are positive and not. When you are positive with the kids, they will want to be in your room. It will be a time of day they look forward to. When students are eager and anticipating your class period, the love that goes back and forth from the kids to the teachers will be generated.

Inspired Phrase 103 Jerry Toups
Those who are able to maintain a positive attitude at all times will soon become an inspiration to others.

Everyone can wake up and CHOOSE to be positive. This is a choice. When you make it a habit, your positivity will inspire those around you, and eventually, this inspiration will turn into love. This love will become a powerful motivator. The difference between compelling others to act through fear of breaking a rule versus love is that love is the basis of your inspiration through the ultimate teacher descriptors. When kids are obedient in your room through love and not through a set of rules, you will develop intrinsically motivated students. This, in turn, will create students who behave, but also who want to learn. One powerful way to develop this love is to just be positive.

Secondly, do you know your students? Do you know each student? Do you know their favorite things, what they like to do? When the kids realize you are getting to know them as an individual, this will generate love. This love does not have a politically correct agenda. Love each individual kid that enters your room. Love is color blind. Love each kid for who they are. Tell each kid they are amazing; they were created to do wonderful things. They are all unique. TELL THEM THIS. Our kids now, more than ever, need to hear their lives will be impactful. Love is generated when you do this in a powerful way.

Third, be empathetic. The letter from my former student Cheyenne is an excellent example of this. Your students need to know you care about them. This is done through non-verbal communication showing them that you have empathy for them. When you have a high school student that gets off a work shift at midnight and then shows up for school the next day, the last thing they need to hear is their teacher griping at them for not doing their homework. The teacher should know the kid's situation then thank them for being there. I have also taught sixth-graders who have the responsibility to get their younger siblings ready for school. So sad that an 11-year-old is the substitute parent in this situation. Show the kid you care about them and do not complain to them. There is a fine line between complaining and encouraging them to be responsible. In the end, you should be thankful the kid has made an effort to show up to your classroom. If you make the room positive and the students want to be in your room, they are likely to share this information with you. The kids will know you care about them. This will generate love.

Fourth, produce a smile. Make your classroom a place where kids want to be. Be a source of happiness each day in their life.

"Mr. Toups
You are, by far, the best teacher I have ever had in my entire life.
Every day I look forward to coming to your class.
ALWAYS BELIEVE – Jerry Maddox"

When you create a smile daily in your student's life, they will look forward to coming to your room. Creating a smile is done largely through verbal communication. Say things that will create a smile. Develop a set of stories you share with your kids through the year that will create a theme of happiness.

I started teaching in 1990. During the mid-90's I was watching <u>Home Improvement</u> and the antics of Tim Allen's Tim the Tool Man Taylor. I thought, "I could do this in my classroom." The kids absolutely love the grunts and the More Power chants. When I tell my

Non-Verbally Communicating Love

"side stories" to the kids, I just pretend I am Tim the Tool Man Taylor, and I put on a show while making the kids smile.

The following is such an example.

"After finding the value that solves the equation, you can always check your answer by substituting the answer into the variable and show how both sides of the equation end up being the same. Hoo hoo hoo hoo hooo." (Tim Taylor grunt) I am closing my lesson on how to solve multi-step equations using the antics of Tim Taylor. "Ashley, doesn't it feel kind of awesome that your answer actually makes the equation a true statement?" Ashley looks at me with a weird kind of face while nodding her head like not really. The other students share similar faces. Math does not make us feel like this. My students are now anticipating a "Toups Story" that will generate a smile.

I then ask a student who is not agreeing with me, "Brian, you don't get all happy and joyful when you solve an equation correctly."

Brian replies, "Not really, Mr. Toups."

I then say, "Class, do you really want to know what it feels like when you start getting really hard math problems correct?" The class is eagerly awaiting the "Toups's Story" I continue talking to my junior high students, "Well, it is like this. Stephanie, let us say you really, really like this boy, but no one else knows you like him. But he is so cute, and he is just such an amazing guy. Well, you go to an assembly into the gym, and the principal is randomly sitting the students, so you don't sit by all your friends, and OMG, you get to sit right next to the boy you have a crush on! Aah ho ho ho (Tim Taylor grunt) What do you say? Do you smile at him? What do you do? While you are trying to think of something to say to your heartthrob, your heart starts beating faster, your back starts getting sweat on it." I continue to go through a descriptive list of what "puppy love" does to you. The kids are all smiling. Then I close the story with, "Guys, you know this feeling, right?" The kid's smiles are an affirmation that they have experienced this feeling of hormonal overload. Then I say with a huge smile, "This is what it will begin to feel like when you solve a math problem correctly. You will get all HOT. You will feel like that moment when you get to sit by the person you have a crush on. It will give you More Power!"

Stories like this are things your kids will remember. Later during the year, when the thermostat is off, and the kids are saying, "Mr. Toups, why is it so hot in your room?" I will say, "Well, you are doing math, and when you do math it makes you feel *hot*?" When it gets too cold in my room and the kids say, "Mr. Toups it's cold in here." In the world of modern schools where you really can't adjust the thermostat, I will reply with, "Well, the administration knows this is a math class, and they know when you do math problems correctly, it makes you feel so *hot*." I refer to this "*hot*" theme frequently during the year, and the smiles produced are priceless. When kids associate you with a smile, this, in turn, will develop into the kids saying you love them. This is another student testimony on how this story impacted them.

"Mr. Toups, I thank you sooo much for being an amazing math teacher. You have taught me so much and helped me out with my papers and grades. I think I would probably know nothing at all about math if it weren't for you. Every day when math is over, you tell us to have an awesome day, and it just makes things better. Also, it is soo funny when someone says it's hot and you say it's because we're thinking about math. Thanks for everything. Jenna"

Perhaps one of the most powerful things a student can say about their teacher is that they love them. This love is truly done non-verbally in a multitude of ways. Among these are being positive, knowing what makes a person unique, showing empathy to others, and just being the source of a daily smile. If you look at the ultimate teacher descriptor diagram, love will truly be the source of inspiring your students. The other descriptors will be generated when the kids know you love them. Love is at the epicenter of inspiration.

Inspired Phrase 809 Jerry Toups
When students know that their teacher loves them unconditionally, their fears and self-doubts will crumble. The students will begin to BELIEVE they can succeed.

Inspired Phrase 942 Jerry Toups
There is no limit to the size of your heart's ability to love others. Your ability to love magnitudes of people has no limits.

Inspired Phrase 66 Jerry Toups
The greatest gift you can give to another person is your love.

Inspired Phrase 41 Jerry Toups
Love someone for who they are, and not what you would like them to be.

Inspired Phrase 684 Jerry Toups
The end result of a teacher's love for their students is not only a child that is academically smarter in the content area, but also a child that is smarter in the lessons of life. The child is a more complete human being.

Inspired Phrase 847 Jerry Toups
Your power to change the lives of others all boils down to your unconditional love for them.

As an educator, there have been years when I have taught 200 plus students per day. Your heart is invigorated when you love your students. There is no limit to the amount of love you can shower on the kids who walk into your room every day. When the kids walk into your room and know they are loved, each day becomes a gift. Every teacher has the power to love every kid in every class. When you do this, your job takes on a different dynamic. You will become a life changer. I would like to close with this parent note. This is another example of how the power of love can connect people with vastly different backgrounds.

"Today, I'm in tears. Happy tears…tears of joy. Muhaymin's favorite teacher of all time and probably the one he will remember forever, came by our house today to give him a book he published about his own adversity and how he overcame it.

He chose three students from 9th grade that put their name in the raffle to receive this book. Muyaymin didn't put his name in, but Mr. Toups came by and gave this to him anyway. He told Muhaymin that he was one of his favorite students this year and that he reminded him of himself as a high schooler.

Muhaymin would always come home, telling me that this teacher was always lifting his spirits when others picked on him. Always telling him to "believe," always telling him that his success doesn't rely on how many friends he has or how popular he is. Such a positive force and attitude coming from someone who was always picked on as a child too. He would share his stories with Muhaymin, and they have had a profound impact on him.

Today was a very emotional day for him, saying that when he is successful in life, he's going to come back to share his success with Mr. Toups. He said this was his happiest day in the past several months.

This is the impact that teachers can have on students when they notice them, when they notice their struggle. Seriously my heart is filled with gratitude towards this man that probably has very little in common with our family. But the love in his heart is what connected a proud Muslim boy to a proud conservative Christian teacher."

JERRY TOUPS, JR.

Jerry Toups, Jr.

Jerry Toups Jr. was raised in the south-east Texas town of Port-Neches. As a child he experienced the many traumas of today's youth, including bullying and gun violence. Mr. Toups graduated from Port-Neches Groves High School in 1985.

Jerry then attended Lamar University in Beaumont, Texas where he was a student athletic trainer. He majored in Health Education desiring a career in the medical field. When selecting a minor, he picked mathematics, a decision that would eventually become his career. He graduated from Lamar University on May 12, 1990 with a Bachelor of Science in Health Education and a minor in mathematics.

During the summer of 1989 Jerry made his first journey away from south-east Texas to Camp Cayuga, a summer camp in the Pocono Mountains of Pennsylvania. It was during this summer that he discovered his talents to inspire and motivate kids and he was coined with the nickname of Tex.

In August of 1990 Jerry would get his first teaching job at Killeen High School. During the staff development in-services before the school year began he was told to create his classroom rules. This is where he inked his first rule as being "Always Believe in Yourself". Since then thousands of middle school and high school students have answered the question, "What is the first rule?" The phrase "Always Believe" had begun to inspire his students.

In the fall of 1992 Jerry moved to Dayton, TX, a rural crossroad town in south-east Texas, where he would teach for the next twenty years, mostly as a junior high math teacher. In 2001 he was voted Teacher of the Year for Woodrow Wilson Junior High. In 2004 he started video-taping and photographing the "Friday Night Lights" of the Dayton Broncos football team, band, drill team, and cheerleaders. It was here that his "Always Believe" theme captivated and inspired the entire community of Dayton, TX.

In the spring of 2013, as if guided by an unseen force, he left everything he had built and moved with his family to Lamar CISD where his "Always Believe" theme was embraced by George Ranch High School. His dream of giving away an "Always Believe Scholarship" became reality, and "Always Believe" helped inspire the students and community to a football state championship in 2015.

In the spring of 2019 Jerry became a published a book, "The Story of Always Believe," which is an inspirational auto-biography of the stories and events that shaped his life and career.

Since 1990 Jerry awakens every day eager to go to work. His career has produced an indescribable positive attitude that impacts not just his students, but also his coworkers.

When you empower others to believe, joy will overcome your soul. Jerry's life story and career is a living tribute to this truth.

14

TO BE YOUNG, GIFTED, TALENTED, AND BLACK

THE STRUGGLES OF BLACK BOYS IN AMERICAN PUBLIC SCHOOLS' SPECIAL EDUCATION PROGRAMS

JASON B. ALLEN

One of the reasons I left administration and returned to the classroom was the high and growing number of Black boys public schools are failing. In fact, having to discipline Black boys in systematic ways made me a part of the system failing Black boys. Public schools are either disproportionately placing Black boys in special education programs or placing them out of school through the school to prison pipeline. The alarming rate of Black boys in either all have stories leading back to experiences Black boys having in general education classrooms.

Most of the Black boys that came through my office have a history of being suspended, ultimately being expelled from school. Even more significantly, the students had deficiencies in their academics, contributing to their behavior problems. Notably, a good number of Black boys who had learning disabilities weren't properly assessed. Their records reflected the school's punitive behavior management. After two years in school administration, I became a Special Education Teacher. In this space, I began working to improve the educational experiences of Black boys in special education programs.

The struggles of Black boys in American public schools start at the elementary level. One contributing factor to their struggle is identity in early development. Not having a Black male teacher Pre- K through fifth grade does negatively impact the educational experiences of Black boys in special education programs. Other organizations like Profound Gentlemen are pushing for more male educators of color to entire classrooms, especially PK-5 classrooms. Improving practices to engage parents of Black boys in early indicators of learning disabilities is a solution. Advocating for public school districts to recruit more male educators of color in the special education field helps improve the educational outcomes of Black boys in special education too.

Supporting parents of Black boys in the SST process in elementary school helps lessen the numbers of Black boys who remain in special education programs for more than three years. My parents had me tested for the gifted and talented program early in elementary school. This is also how they found out that I was dual exceptional. It was both my parents and teachers that also caught early that I had developed a learning disability. Testing and implementing best practices early helps decrease the high numbers of Black boys in special education programs. It sounds much easier than it is. Barriers such as a teacher shortage, not enough resources, and overcrowded classrooms attributes to the matriculation of Black boys in special education programs.

Black boys aren't the only group disproportionately represented in special education classrooms. So are Black male educators. According to the Center for Black Educators Development, only 2% of Black males make up 20% of Black teachers in the profession. Currently, Black male educators are five times more likely to leave the education profession than other groups. The area of special education follows early childhood education in lacking the presence of male educators of color and also having the highest numbers of them to leave the classroom. I have seen this data live and in color. I have been in several school districts in Metro Atlanta, where I was the only Black male teacher in the special education department and sometimes the school. Black boys who weren't on my special education caseload showed up to my co-taught classes. I taught Black boys in special education throughout various grade levels how to improve on their goals. None of the Black boys in the program knew what their goals were. It's possible they hadn't been informed or hadn't communicated the goals effectively. I can't speak directly to previous teachers' intent, but I know that I spend extra time cleaning up the mistakes and gaps in Black boys IEPS than any other student on my classloads. The negligence displayed in their records speaks volumes about the level of effective service they were provided. I believe this contributes to their abilities to not only get effective services but gain the progress needed on their goals.

Black boys are struggling academically, socially, and emotionally in special education programs. The National Center of Education Statistics reflects that 14%, 7.1 million American students are in Special education programs. Of that, 9% of those students are Black boys. The disproportionate number of Black boys in special education programs is drastically high and alarming. Currently, I'm in my Masters of Special Education program. Several of the assigned articles we've read have lacked substantive best practices to improve the educational outcomes of Black boys who are going through the special education programs. Systemic racism, prejudices about students with disabilities, and stereotypes of Black boys all play a role in their experiences in special education.

Black boys are struggling to show progress in special education programs academically. It's almost like the pandemic. We're simply experimenting on the right vaccine and stabilizing as best as we can until then. Public schools are just working to stabilize special education programs. Black boys, in my perspective, are being experimented on to figure out which medicines for such as ADHD, ADD, anxiety, and other emotional and behavioral disabilities that Black boys are diagnosed with, including Autism. Black boys are exploited by schools for additional dollars for federal program funding while allowing them to coast through school. Coasting but not excelling. Coasting but not filling in the academic gaps that attribute to their exceptionalities. In my Special Education in Regular Classrooms course, a lot of the focus is on the laws and practicalities of services for special education programs. I think this is a help and hindrance. A hindrance because too often, there's more focus on the law than teaching and learning.

I've observed that what's being taught in teacher education programs impacts how special education programs are facilitated. If we're training special education teachers to simply follow the law and not how to implement best practices to improve the outcomes of Black boys with exceptionalities, then we'll continue failing Black boys in special education programs. Other dynamics, such as the teacher shortage, contribute to how Black boys perform academically. In one school district, I filled a vacant special education that was unoccupied for three years. I've moved on to another school district, and that position is still vacant. The lack of teachers doesn't allow public schools to fully service Black boys in special education programs. Vast challenges in virtual learning platforms are attributing to more academic complications for Black boys too. For example, Black boys with ADHD and Dyslexia have deficiencies in literacy. Virtual learning is a lot more literacy online without having the know-how of a teacher to break information down or reteach. Reteaching strategies is a solution in reducing the academic struggles of Black boys in special education. Although this is a solution, it's difficult for special education teachers to provide this virtually. Whether it's the exceptionality, the lack of teachers, resources, or effective teaching practices, Black boys aren't performing academically as they could be in special education programs. It's important to address this and reflect that it's not simply the exceptionalities of Black boys that prevent some from obtaining academic success.

The lack of Black identity impacts how Black boys perform academically. At an early age, I learned the importance of having a voice and using it. I teach the Black boys on my caseload to advocate for the services they need in special education programs. Public schools too often silence Black boys in special education classrooms. This lack of connection stems from the inability of SPED program coordinators and teachers to identify with Black boys. Because they aren't able to connect with them, the implementation of award based programs is used to get Black boys to succeed academically. Filling the lack of black identity involves hearing Black boys' voices in special education classrooms across America. According to Ed Week, the majority of American educators are middle-class white women. The majority of school board leaders in American cities are conservative white men. That doesn't sound quite like a recipe of success for Black boys who have been racially discriminated against in the history of American schools. Special education programs are exempt from racial discrimination. Black identity in public schools is vitally important to Black boys' success in general and special education classrooms.

Social and emotional programs don't align with Black boys' needs to thrive and survive in our society. Black males aren't in the positions to attribute to Black boys' successes in special education programs. The physical therapists, psychologists, social workers, and counselors are more often than not Black males. Black boys are socially battling the stereotypes of students labeled as exceptional learners. Emotionally they are battling trauma, neglect from home and school, fear of failure, and anxiety. Research from the Fordham Institute displays data speaking to the impact of identity in social and emotional development of students. Black boys in special education classrooms need strong social and emotional support too. Often, the specialists, i.e. occupational or physical therapists, counselors, social workers, and even behavior interventionists, don't have the capacity to meet all the social and emotional needs of Black boys. I have seen Black boys fail out of school from being in special education programs for years. They haven't filled in academic gaps and haven't successfully developed emotionally or socially. So many of them are victims of the social injustices we see in our society. The lack of equitable resources and the effectiveness of services that should be provided to Black boys doesn't just show up academically, but in the social and emotional growth and development of Black boys as well. For Black boys fighting against societal pressures to be the tough guy or the bad boy, having a disability makes this challenging. So Black boys resort to poor behaviors that take the focus away from their peers that they struggle with learning. Psychologically this does something to Black boys. Some Black boys feel trapped socially and emotionally due to the fear of being stereotyped as dumb, slow, or less than others. The anxiety Black boys are dealing with isn't discussed or even considered in professional development. I believe it's because for so long public schools have been positioned to focus on the behaviors of Black boys and failing to meet their social and emotional needs. The numbers of Black boys in public schools in educational programs reflect that most of them have IEPs with an ADD and ADHD diagnosis, which comes with medications. Medications to help with behaviors and anxiety. Anxiety created an atmosphere personified through a reality of hopelessness Black boys experience by acting out to avoid many schools' general negligence to support them socially and emotionally.

Although there are many challenges Black boys face in special education, I believe school districts can implement solutions. One solution is advocating for state programs to diversify the teacher pipeline. If Black boys are disproportionately represented in special education programs and male educators of color in special education classrooms, finding ways to get more teachers who look like them in classrooms may help. Identity and representation have been sited by the Center of Black Educators to help Black boys excel academically. Organizations such as Profound Gentlemen (PG) work to recruit and retain male educators of color in classrooms and public schools. PG highlights that 2% of male educators of color in classrooms are growing despite the teacher shortage and the pandemic. I've been supported by both organizations when I had little support from the public school districts. I may be one teacher in the 2%, but I know that Black boys need more male educators of color in special education classrooms to help bring much-needed growth and change.

JASON B. ALLEN

Jason B. Allen

Jason B. Allen is a Special Education teacher in Georgia. Jason has worked in Education for over fifteen (15) years as a teacher and leader servicing students, families and communities. He uses he platform to empower Black male educators to advocate for social justice through his work with Profound Gentlemen. As an education activist and blogger (EdLanta), Jason actively speaks and writes on ways to improve educational outcomes. He is a member of the Association of American Educators (AAE) and an AAE Foundation Advocacy Fellow.

15

NAVIGATING FALL 2020 AND BEYOND
AN ORGANIZATIONAL FRAMEWORK TO NAVIGATE BETWEEN ONLINE, BLENDED, AND TRADITIONAL EDUCATIONAL SETTINGS

MATTHEW C. RHOADS, ED.D.

An organizational framework must be in place throughout the 2020-2021 school year and beyond to help districts and schools navigate online, blended, and traditional educational settings during the COVID-19 pandemic. Learning and instruction can be continuous during this unprecedented time.

As the 2020-2021 school year began, K-12 schools continued to reassess how instruction will occur with social distancing, staggered schedule, and hygienic protocols in place on campus. Furthermore, in order for schools to reopen in some capacity for face to face instruction, critical evaluations and planning needed to occur to determine what type of organizational framework needs to be in place to ensure this happens. At the same time, schools had to think into the future with the fear of having to physically close down once again if the second wave of COVID-19 will inevitably hit in the fall, winter, spring, or if a positive cluster of cases occurs within a school site or district causing it to have to shut down on-campus learning temporarily at any time during the school year. If these scenarios occur in the future, it will result in what has been coined the "toggled term" for K-12 education (Alexander, 2020; Rhoads, 2020). The genesis of the toggled term came from Dr. Bryan Alexander, an education futurist who alluded to this being a possibility for colleges and universities during the fall of 2020. From what we have seen during the 2020-2021 school year, it is inevitable that this "toggled term" will also be the reality in K-12 education for the foreseeable future because of the subsequent physical school closures that have taken place throughout the world (Alexander, 2020). As we have seen so far in the state of Georgia in August 2020, South Korea, Israel, and several European nations who have reopened schools in the spring, schools initially reopened physically. They then had to be closed for the short term or an unforeseen amount of time due to local transmission of COVID-19 on school campuses. As a result, in each instance, schools moved back to online instruction until it was deemed safe by local health authorities to reopen physical schools once again (BBC, 2020).

The Framework - Fullan and Quinn's Coherence Framework

Having a workable framework in place to develop future plans to be ahead of the positive cases inevitably happening within schools will help districts and schools initially physically reopen their doors and then continue to reassess their capacity to toggle back and forth between in-person blended learning and fully online instruction throughout the school year. One successful framework that stands out for school reform is Michael Fullan and Joanne Quinn's (2016) Coherence Framework (as seen in motion below in *Figure 1*), which can be applied to the threat of a toggled term to ensure schools can safely navigate the instructional challenges posed by the pandemic. Fullan and Quinn's framework has transformed districts and schools throughout North America because it allows for the flexibility of local conditions to be integrated into the framework's structural components. From Long Beach, California, to schools in Ontario, Canada, this framework has bolstered completely different districts to move towards higher achievement and better outcomes for their students through the cultural and structural changes outlined in the framework.

Fundamentally, Fullan and Quinn (2016) argue the components of a focused direction, internal and external accountability, cultivating collaborative cultures, and the 6C's of deep learning, which includes citizenship, character, collaboration, creativity, critical thinking, and communication are critical to school reform. When all of these components are in place, they can be the drivers of change so that all teachers and school leaders "have a shared depth of understanding about the purpose and nature" of school reform, which must happen throughout the year to navigate the toggled term (p. 14). Thus, the reality is clear. To navigate the toggled term, a school reform framework is needed to develop plans to physically reopen and then have the organizational and instructional capacity to sustain continuous learning and instruction while intermittently toggling between online, blended, and traditional educational settings based on local health conditions throughout the school year.

Focused Direction. For the first step in formulating this framework, districts and schools must plan to have a purpose in why they are implementing new protocols like social distancing, staggered scheduling, blended learning, and hygienic protocols for when schools reopen. Communicating the purpose to all school stakeholders and the local community will be one of the single most important strategies to ensure everyone is informed of what is going on and why it occurs. The overarching purpose of "why" needs to be accompanied by a clear strategy outlining goals, measuring those goals, and protocols for how a district and school can reopen as well as toggle back and forth between online, blended, and traditional settings, which will depend on local health conditions.

Collaborative Cultures. The second step of this framework that can be adopted involves building capacity through on-going professional development and professional learning networks, collaborative work as grade levels, departments, and entire schools, and accepting that this will be a time of learning and growth (Fullan & Quinn, 2016). In this environment, collaboration among teachers and administrators will be key to developing innovative instruction to create the best learning conditions for our students in online, blended, or traditional educational settings. Teachers need to collaborate virtually and in-person in addition to having a high sense of collective efficacy to experiment and share how they are teaching to others in their local school community as well as their education professional learning network. Leaders, as well as teachers, must motivate others within their community to take instructional risks with educational technology as well as aligning the technology by driving it forward to meet the needs of their students with effective instructional strategies.

Internal/External Accountability. The third step of the framework is securing internal and external accountability from teachers, staff, administrators, and the surrounding community is predicated on the moral imperative. The moral imperative is an overarching culture where all stakeholders, including teachers, buy-in, and belief in the vision as well as initiatives to enact instructional and organizational school policy (Fullan & Quinn, 2016). An example of a moral imperative for our current situation would be buy-in towards utilizing various educational technology tools to deliver instruction like a learning management system(s) and student collaboration, engagement, and assessment tools to enhance learning.

Overall, Fullan and Quinn's (2016) moral imperative is needed to ensure internal and external accountability of all stakeholders in our current scenario of navigating reopening schools and moving back and forth between online, blended, and traditional classroom settings. It establishes an overarching purpose, motivating teachers and leaders to work together to navigate the instruction and organizational challenges presented by our current times.

Deep Learning. The last aspect of this framework to integrate into developing reopening plans and instruction frameworks to navigate online, blended, and traditional classroom settings for our districts and schools are focusing on deep learning. With blended learning in play as one of the most viable instructional models to be utilized during a toggled term, it can be the overarching form of instruction that can then teach the competencies embodied within deep learning. Deep learning fundamentally is taking knowledge from experience and incorporates it across a range of skills and attributes, which include communication, critical thinking, collaboration, creativity, character, and citizenship (Fullan & Quinn, 2016, p. 89-90). Ultimately, incorporating the 6C's can allow primary and secondary schools to engage and instruct students in deep learning in online, blended, and traditional school settings.

Blended Learning & Face to Face Instruction	The "Toggle"	Fully Online Instruction
- Face to face and online instruction - Social Distancing - Hyper Hygiene Practices - Staggered Scheduling	Opening/Closing of Physical Campuses The Coherence Framework in the Context of the Toggled Term - Focused Direction - Internal/External Accountability - Moral Imperative - Deep Learning Instruction is always occurring. The "toggle" is dictated by local health conditions. ← →	- Online instruction only - Temporary until health conditions improve - All instructional platforms and content will always be online just in case a toggle occurs where schools have to close facilities

Figure 1. Navigating 2020 and Beyond Using Fullan and Quinn's (2016) Coherence Framework

How to Best Support Teachers Navigate the Toggled Term

Teachers in 2020-2021 can be best supported by having school and district leaders provide professional development for common instructional language, pedagogical practices, and COVID protocols throughout the school year. Fullan and Quinn (2016) recommend horizontal and vertical professional development across the entire school system to create organizational transparency and capacity before any implementation of these practices occurs. In this same instance, during a time of continuous change, Fullan and Quinn (2016) suggest fostering instructional risk-taking to innovate and improve to create the best outcomes for students as possible. Districts and schools need to allow teachers and administrators to explore and find solutions together at the school site level for the instructional challenges that occur by creating an instructional culture where risk-taking and innovation are encouraged. Ultimately, togetherness and cohesion among teachers and administrators will be key to facilitating the Coherence framework, which will help all members of the school community navigate the challenges of the toggled term created by the COVID-19 pandemic.

Afterword

Fullan and Quinn's Coherence Framework is a start to thinking about how districts and schools must adjust their organizational systems to withstand the realities presented by the toggled term, which may extend beyond the 2020-2021 school year. Frameworks like Fullan and Quinn's can be considered because they are flexible to the local challenges and variables districts and schools may face. Other frameworks may exist that can provide districts and schools with flexibility like this one. However, other frameworks should contain elements like Fullan and Quinn's that provide for a purposeful and focused direction, accountability held together by a moral imperative, collaborative culture to problem solve and innovate, and deep learning propelled by a blended learning and online instructional model that is aligned with the six competencies of 21st-century learning. Frameworks like this will not only prepare us for what's coming in the future, but will put teachers in the driver's seat to place students in the best positions to succeed regardless of the educational setting we are providing instruction throughout the 2020-2021 school year.

References

Alexander, B. (2020). *Early signs of fall 2020: Three paths, three scenarios for higher education.* Retrieved 5 May 2020, from https://bryanalexander.org/

BBC News. (2020). *South Korea closes schools again as cases jump.* Retrieved 4 June 2020, from https://www.bbc.com/news/world-asia-52845015

Fullan, M., Senge, P. M. (2010). *All systems go: The change imperative for whole system reform.* Thousand Oaks: Corwin.

Fullan, M., & Quinn, J. (2016). *Coherence: The right drivers in action for schools, districts, and systems.* Thousand Oaks, CA: Corwin.

Rhoads, M. (2020). *Navigating the toggled term: Preparing Secondary Educators for Navigating Fall 2020 and Beyond.* Bellevue, WA: Amazon Publishing.

Matthew C. Rhoads, Ed.D., is an Educational Specialist, university lecturer, consultant, and author from San Diego, California, who specializes in educational technology and instruction, data-driven decision-making, data literacy, and online and blended learning settings. His new book Navigating the Toggled Term: Preparing Secondary Educators for Navigating Fall 2020 and Beyond focuses on instructional and organizational frameworks that can help K-12 schools and districts toggle between online, hybrid, and traditional educational settings in addition to providing chapters on selecting edtech tools, edtech tools and their instructional applications, differentiating instruction, and online Special Education case management. Dr. Rhoads research interests include teacher and school leader data-driven decision-making, developing data literacy curriculum to teach educators to harness the data collected from edtech to drive instructional decision-making, effective instructional use of edtech tools, and professional development. For more information on Dr. Rhoads, his work, publications, and blog can be found at www.matthewrhoads.com.

16
SIX PRINCIPLES FOR A ROBUST TECHNOLOGY INTEGRATION PLAN

DAWN CARRERA BERKELEY

This chapter explores a few principles from the business world to identify components of a healthy technology integration plan.

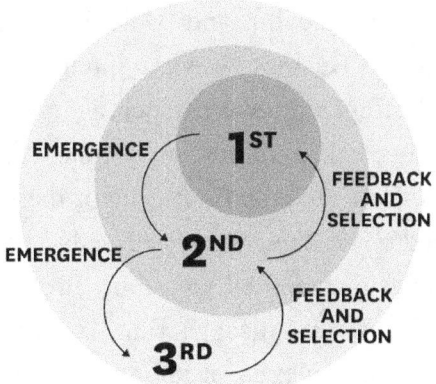

LEVEL	NATURE	BUSINESS
First	**THE POPULATION** Individual organisms of the same species	**THE COMPANY** Individual employees
Second	**THE NATURAL ECOSYSTEM** Populations of species that depend on and compete with one another	**THE BUSINESS ECOSYSTEM** Companies that depend on and compete with one another
Third	**THE BROADER NATURAL ENVIRONMENT** Neighboring ecosystems and nonbiological elements, such as the climate	**THE BUSINESS ENVIRONMENT** Overlapping ecosystems and other stakeholders, such as NGOs, government entities, and civil society

From "The Biology of Corporate Survival," January–February 2016 © HBR.ORG

Originally, I was thinking of penning this post, "Survival of the Fittest for Your Tech Integration Strategy." Read more to find out why. As a former biology teacher turned tech integrator, I found Martin Reeves, Simon Levin, and Daichi Ueda's recent article featured in the Harvard Business Review interesting. The Biology of Corporate Survival offers a unique perspective on what causes corporations to fail or succeed, juxtaposed with survival principles from natural ecosystems. You can also find some of these ideas revealed in Reeves' co-authored book, Your Strategy Needs a Strategy.

The writers investigated 30,000 public firms in the US. They concluded that businesses are disappearing like never before for their failure to adapt to the complexity of their environment. If we were to align this idea to our various school contexts, we could then pose the question of why technology integration efforts fail? In what ways do we anticipate, build and sustain complexity?

Their research takes a rather interesting look at the intersectionality between business strategy, biology, and complex systems and what makes each of the systems more robust. The more biologically diverse an environment and ecosystem are, the better their chances of natural survival and sustainability. Additionally, it is known that diverse, healthy ecosystems can better withstand and recover from various disasters. The writers refer to these systems as "complex adaptive systems." In this vein, not only are businesses and biological species complex adaptive systems (CAS), but so are schools.

In a complex adaptive system, the interactions between local events and organisms shape the system, resulting in a never-ending feedback loop, where systems are influenced by the individuals and the individuals by the system. Such systems are nested in broader systems — i.e., teachers and students are nested in broader systems of school and local culture.

The authors propose six (6) principles that make a CAS robust, and I would argue the same in light of technology integration efforts. In the future, my plan is to tackle each one of these in the context of technology adoption and integration within schools. When I originally penned this post in 2016, the imminent threat of a global pandemic was not something many educators considered. Since March of this year, the consideration and development of the robust systems and structures I refer to in the post have become even more critically important. In the future, my plan is to examine each of the following principles in what has commonly been referred to as the "new normal." I hope you will join me on this journey as I try to make sense of this.

As Reeves et al. see it, here are those six principles:

1. maintain heterogeneity of people, ideas, and endeavors
2. sustain a modular structure
3. preserve redundancy among components
4. expect surprise, but reduce uncertainty

5. create feedback loops and adaptive mechanisms
6. foster trust and reciprocity in their business ecosystems

References

Life. (2014, January 19). Why is Biodiversity Important? Who cares? – global issues. Retrieved May 9, 2016, from http://www.globalissues.org/article/170/why-is-biodiversity-important-who-cares.

Reeves, M., Levin, S., & Ueda, D. (2016, January 1). The biology of corporate survival. Retrieved May 9, 2016, from Managing uncertainty, https://hbr.org/2016/01/the-biology-of-corporate-survival.

Science for designers: Complex Adaptive Systems – Point of View – August 2012. (2012, August 6). Retrieved May 9, 2016, from http://www.metroplismag.com/Point-of-View/August-2012/Science-for-Designers-Complex-Adaptive-Systems/ Retrieved May 9, 2016

Six Principles for a Robust Technology Integration Plan

The importance of opportunity and equal access to education was instilled in Dawn Berkeley as a young girl. That is why she has devoted the past 20 years of her career to championing the power of technology to transform teaching and learning. As a passionate advocate for accessible education, she has developed creative, inclusive, flexible, and diverse technology-based educational interventions and structures in the public and private sector.

Dawn is the Director of Educational Technology at St. Albans School in Washington, DC. Here, she develops overall vision frameworks for accessible learning and supports educators and students in the training and implementation of learning technologies. Before this, she spent 15+ years in secondary level education as a science teacher and in various capacities as school Technological Coordinator.

Her Independent EdTech Consultancy offers technology skills training and development for children **and** adults. Workshops are based on topics such as 'Digital Animation with Scratch' and 'Google Classroom for Educators and Students'. Her most popular parenting seminars on tech help parents navigate the digital landscape with their teens. She has also developed an extensive list of in-person and online courses including 'Mobile Device policies', 'Mindful Tech Use' and 'Exploring Online Teaching'.

Dawn completed her B.S. Biology degree at the University of Maryland in 2000. In 2012 she earned an M.S. Education, Instructional Media & Technology at Wilkes University in 2012. She holds certifications as a Raspberry Pi and Google Level 1 and 2 Educator and has previously had a role on the Leadership Council of the Discovery Educators Network (DEN). Recently, she completed the coveted International Society for Technology Education (ISTE) certification which empowers her to help PK-12 educators rethink and redesign learning activities with technology to engage students in real-world, authentic, active learning.

When she is not developing ways to make learning more engaging for educators and students, she volunteers at several Raspberry Pi, Scratch and STEM activities and festivals. Her downtime is spent with her family, traveling, hiking, appreciating modern art, or helping her four children make sense of the world.

17

POSITIVE MATH TALK

ALICE ASPINALL

Words are powerful - let's use them to enable mathematics learning.

It Begins at Home

North America has become a society of people who think it is cool - even trendy - to hate math. I have heard the words, "I am not a math person," or similar so many times that I now cringe at the statement. I find myself urging people to give math another chance as an adult because we are all capable of learning math.

I hear the same message from frustrated parents year after year, "I was never good at math, so I'm not expecting [my child] to be great at it." If your child has been hearing this message since they were young, I think they would begin to believe it eventually.

You will often hear me using this analogy: I am a mother to a daughter. I have read many messages urging mothers to be careful with the language they use when addressing body image in front of their daughters – we don't want to portray our bodies negatively, which could perpetuate onto our young daughters' minds.

Can we liken this idea to how we discuss math around our young children?

For some reason, our generation learned to hate math from a young age, and now we are making the mistake of perpetuating those feelings onto our children. We would never tell our children that we can't read, so why are we so quick to tell them we can't do math? There has been a lot of work lately to change the math narrative, and we can all play a part in this.

The current generation of parents holds many people who hate math. We were brought up to believe that "math people" exist, and only these people, with this innate talent, can comprehend the subject. Thankfully, the idea of the "math person" has been proven untrue through the work of Dr. Jo Boaler and her team at Stanford University, YouCubed. We now know that there is no such thing as a math person and that we are all born with the ability to learn math.

Change begins with our vocabulary. Changing the words we use with our children around learning math can drastically change our own mindset and their mindsets about math. The image below shows some suggestions for how we can reframe our thoughts when working with children.

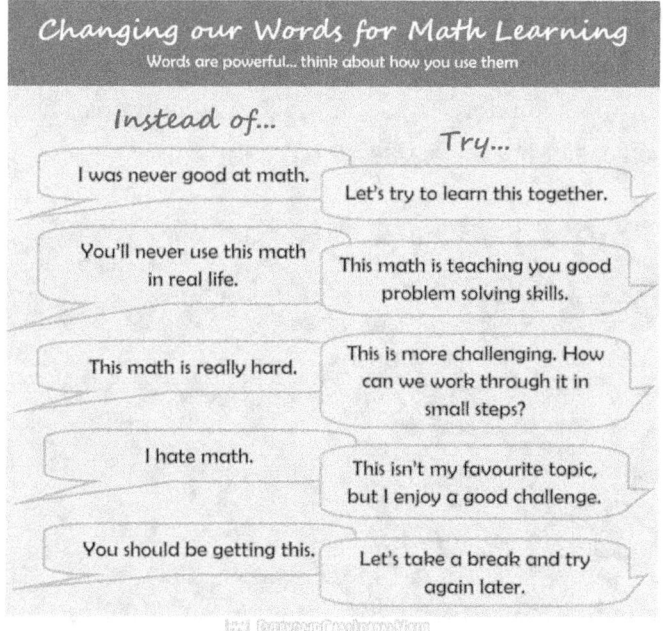

It can be difficult to reframe our thinking when we carry strong feelings of anxiety and angst about a topic, as many do about math, but we need to remember how children pick up on our actions, emotions, and words and mimic what we do. We don't want the next generation to grow up with the same math anxiety that exists in society today, so we need to make deliberate changes to prevent it.

Math anxiety often begins at a very young age and usually is associated with homework. Children and parents continue to find themselves frustrated with math work that is sent home to be completed. The difference lies in how we handle situations where our child experiences struggle with learning math for the first time. Instead of defaulting to the tempting response of, "I was always bad at math, too," I encourage you to try something different. Perhaps we can respond with, "This wasn't my best subject, but maybe we can learn it together." I think this sends the message that it is okay to struggle, but we can always try to improve ourselves, even if it takes some hard work. There is no better way to show our children they can learn something new than by learning it with them. The next time you find yourself in this situation, try some of the suggestions below to help facilitate an easier homework session.

Positive Math Statements
use your words to motivate our children to learn math

You used to struggle with this, but now you are really getting it!	Math is a worthwhile challenge.	Let's try to connect this problem to a real-life scenario.
Let's work on this problem together.	If we practice a little more, I think you will feel more confident.	There is no such thing as a math person.
I believe in you. I know you can do this!	I never learned this well; could I try to learn it again with you?	I think we should try a different approach.
Meditating could help us clear our minds.	This math is really fun and interesting!	Time to take a break; we can try again later.

EVERYONE CAN LEARN MATH

In being deliberate about choosing positive wording when talking about math at home, our children have a better chance of developing positive feelings around learning math and are less likely to develop math anxiety.

We are all trying our best when it comes to raising our children. We want to see them experience success, especially in those things we may not have felt successful in. Let's all try to build a generation that is not afraid of math. It begins at home.

Five Tips for Incorporating a Growth Mindset into the Math Classroom

Growth mindset has become very popular in education and is, in a way, a bit of a buzz term. However, the benefits of applying growth mindset strategies in the math classroom have been visible among most of my students in my secondary mathematics classroom. I am a strong advocate for shifting our teaching from fixed mindset approaches to incorporating a growth mindset. Below are five ways teachers can build a positive math mindset into their classrooms. In my experience, these ideas have worked successfully, having implemented an intentional growth mindset classroom since 2016.

1. Pay Attention to your Vocabulary

The words we choose when speaking to students is one of the most powerful tools we have at our disposal for developing a growth mindset. Changing our vocabulary from fixed mindset language to growth mindset language has been proven to help our students believe they can learn math, which in turn increases their willingness to try something new.

Earlier, we addressed the influence parents have on their children regarding their language framed around math. However, it is just as important for us, as educators, to also be aware of the words we use around children of all ages. Words can either motivate or discourage a child from reaching their potential in a classroom.

The same examples of positive math language apply to us as educators in the classroom, no matter the age or subject matter we teach. Try substituting common negative language used concerning math with positive language instead.

2. Believe in your Students' Abilities

Our students know when we believe in their potential to be successful. It is important to tell our students frequently and explicitly that we think they are good mathematicians. Focus on praising the effort and the process rather than the final result, and your students will begin to believe in themselves as much as we do.

In *Mathematical Mindsets* (2016), Jo Boaler references a study done in high school English classes where hundreds of students wrote essays and received feedback. Half the students were given an extra sentence at the end of their feedback, "I am giving you this feedback because I believe in you." A year later, the students who were given the extra sentence were still performing at higher levels than those who had not.

Students can sense when we want them to do well, but let's take it a step further and make it clear that we believe in them and know they can learn mathematics.

3. Embrace Mistakes as Growth

Creating an atmosphere in our classrooms that allows students to take risks ensures that students will start problems without the fear of making mistakes. There is a misconception among students that they should just "get" math the first time they are taught it, and when they make a mistake, they feel discouraged.

When we think of learning anything new in our lives, we very rarely know how to do something the first time we try without making any mistakes. An example that always comes to mind is when my daughter was learning to skip rope. She tried over and over again, at first only skipping once or twice over the rope before it got tangled in her feet. However, she persisted. She set small goals for herself. First, she tried to get three jumps in a row, then five, and so on. Can we help our students apply this same mindset to learning mathematics?

We do not need to solve a problem on the first try, but we need to be willing to embrace the mistakes and learn from them. I have seen this list for embracing mistakes all over the internet recently, and I think it is a thorough summary of how we need to view mistakes in the classroom.

The other important part of embracing mistakes is to model a growth mindset ourselves as educators. We cannot expect our students to be open to learning if we are not setting the same example.

. . .

4. Offer Multiple Opportunities for Assessment

Mistakes are to be embraced when learning mathematics. We need our students to know that if they make mistakes, they will have more opportunities to show that they have corrected their mistakes and learned from them. Therefore, it is important to offer our students multiple chances to show their learning. This is why re-assessments play a necessary role in the growth mindset classroom.

I feel very strongly that students should be allowed re-assessments, no matter the grade level, because the goal is to learn a concept, not to have learned it the first time they are assessed. In my experience, re-assessments, especially at the secondary level, are met with a lot of resistance. I think this is because we have become very grade focused. If we refocus – both ourselves and our students – on the learning process, instead of the outcome, we can place more value on learning from our mistakes, thus opening the door to re-assessing when students have had a chance to fix and learn from their previous errors.

5. Listen to your Students' Feelings

Although we want our students to have a growth mindset when learning math instead of thinking they are just "bad at math," it is still important to acknowledge students' feelings toward math. Math anxiety is a real thing for many people, and we do not want to dismiss those feelings.

On the first day of the semester, I ask my new students to anonymously answer the question "How do you feel about math?" on a piece of paper. When everyone is finished, we crumple up our papers and toss them across the classroom (you may know this as a "Snowball" activity). Each student picks up a random paper and opens it up. We then take turns reading the answers aloud, knowing that all the papers have been randomized. Not surprisingly, in grades 9 and 10, I see mostly negative feelings associated with mathematics. We talk about how we will work toward improving our math abilities during the semester. Students feel empowered to know that their feelings have been acknowledged and are being considered in the structure of our classroom. I usually save all the responses until the last day of class, and we do the same activity all over again. It is amazing to hear changes in math attitudes, even if only slight.

By acknowledging our students' negative emotions around math, we show them that their feelings are valid and important. We also have a starting point toward changing those math attitudes.

Implementing explicit growth mindset strategies in my classroom over the past four years has drastically changed my students' attitudes toward learning math, leaving them with increased confidence and more willingness to learn. I think this should be the goal of the mathematics classroom – not just to produce high grades – but to encourage students to want to learn and improve themselves.

Keep spreading the math love <3

References

Boaler, J., & Dweck, C. S. (2016). Mathematical mindsets: unleashing students potential through creative math, inspiring messages and innovative teaching. San Francisco, CA: Jossey-Bass.

YouCubed. (2020). Retrieved from https://www.youcubed.org/

Alice Aspinall

Alice Aspinall, B.Math(Hon), B.Ed, is a Portuguese-Canadian secondary mathematics educator in Ontario, Canada. She is a strong advocate of the growth mindset and is continually looking for ways to build young people's confidence in math and to make math fun, challenging, and satisfying. Alice is also a champion for females in STEM by encouraging girls to pursue science and mathematics both in high school and in post-secondary education. Alice believes everyone can learn math and she is on a mission to prove it. She is the author of the children's book, *Everyone Can Learn Math*.

Alice has over 12 years of experience teaching secondary mathematics, over 6 years tutoring elementary and secondary mathematics privately, and 4 years teaching elementary mathematics in small groups in schools. She also holds an Honour Specialist in Mathematics and an additional qualification in Special Education, Part I.

18

MATHREPS

LISA M. NOWAKOWSKI

Help students gain math muscle memory several standards at a time.

MathReps Beginning

Many years ago, I watched in amazement as a friend, Jon Corippo, spoke about a protocol (later EduProtocol) called 8 p*ARTS of Speech. In short, he taught all eight parts of speech at once in a fun and engaging way. He taught all them for eight weeks instead of breaking them apart a week at a time. I thought this was brilliant and immediately wanted to create something like this for math.

By this time, I had been teaching 5th grade for several years, and I noticed that by the time the end of the year came, students hadn't had enough spiral review of the concepts taught at the beginning of the year. Aside from the root causes being many, this was also creating gaps in students' learning and progress. This was an issue I desperately wanted to help fix.

MathReps Were Born

Shortly after being inspired, I began to create the first MathRep. A reality check quickly followed. Unlike the original inspiration that could work for several grade levels, math was a different ball game. Each grade level has differing standards that build upon each other. I soon realized that I had to create various collections for each grade level.

I set about thinking about the most crucial math standards my students needed to know. That was not an easy task. If you teach math, you know that each concept feels so incredibly important. What I ended up with was a page of 8-10 standards the students could review daily. The best part of it was that I only needed to change one number. The number of the day could be manipulated to fit all the standards. My students were not only up for the task but saw the benefits of this new protocol.

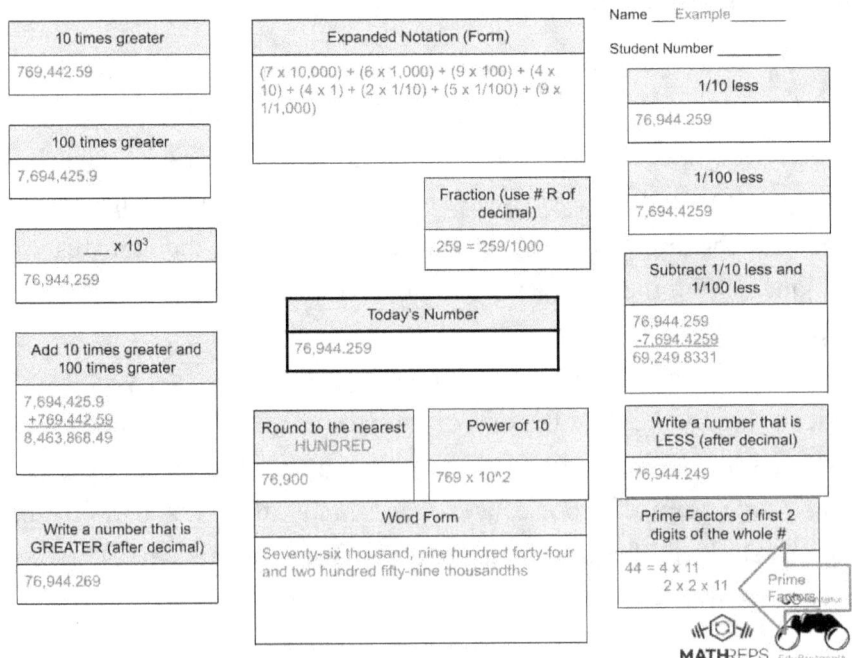

Results

The first time I introduced MathReps to my students, it took 45 minutes to complete. Yes, banging my head against a brick wall would have been less painful. But guess what? By Friday of that week, we had it down to 15 minutes. There were even some students who wanted to go ahead because they knew what to do. Their proficiency increased, as did their confidence. As the year progressed, I introduced new MathReps: multiplication and division, multiplication and division with decimals, and fractions. I have a vivid memory of one student working through division. In the 5th grade, the area model is the standard. It's not until sixth grade students are expected to know the standard algorithm. However, one day I noticed one particular student working through a division problem and not using the area model but what looked like a hybrid of the area model and the standard algorithm. I stopped a moment and asked him to explain his process. He happily explained that the way he was doing it was easier for him and made more sense. I further probed if anyone had shown him, and he said that he noticed the patterns on his own. This is what we want in math: students making connections, seeing patterns, and making the natural progressions to advance their learning. We want students to take ownership of their education. That is precisely what happened!

Another year we were reviewing previously learned concepts. It was the end of the year, and my team chose standards from the beginning of the year to review in preparation for the state test. One particular problem dealt with adding/subtracting decimals. Afterward, another teacher and I compared notes on where the students had issues and successes. The teacher found that her students were confused by the decimal and didn't remember to line them up when adding/subtracting. I found that interesting and began to wonder what the difference was between our classes. I then went back to my class and discussed the difference. As we had built a culture of respect towards all, we were able to focus on the difference in our approach as opposed to a competitive 'one class did better than another' discussion. I asked my class what the difference could be. One student pointed out, "You make us do MathReps every day, and that [adding/subtracting decimals] was on there." And they were right! It was the repetition that helped my students remember the concept.

The Movement Begins

Upon creating the first MathRep, I wrote a blog post about it and tagged Jon. Shortly after that post, I saw him at a conference, and he pulled me aside to explain what I had done with another educator. Jon was not only excited; he was a fan. He loved the iteration and began sharing the idea with others.

As a result, others started creating them and sharing with me. This was a blessing. While I love math and understand the standards, it was hard for me to think about creating something for all grades, especially middle school and high school MathReps. Because of the sharing culture that so many educators have, I now had something for every grade level. Then, the movement continued to spread when Jon Corippo and Marlena Hebern, co-authors of EduProtocol Field Guide books 1 and 2, shared MathReps in book 1, on their webpage, and during presentations.

As word spread and more MathReps were created, a core group of people began to develop and share. Not only were people sharing with me, but MathReps were making their way to various platforms such as Google Slides, Jamboard, Nearpod, Pear Deck, and SeeSaw.

Any good movement these days gets active on social media. MathReps is no different. We now have a Facebook page, group, hashtag, and a website (mathreps.com).

How it Works

The idea is simple: introduce the MathReps to the class and work through it together for approximately a week. By the end of the week, you will have several students who will begin to work ahead. If you are using the paper/pencil method, copy the form on both sides. This way, students can refer to the backside for a reminder. Beginning in the second week of MathReps, allow students to work on it independently. I also allow students to talk to one another for help. I set a time limit to keep us all on track. I allow 8 - 12 minutes depending on the MathRep assigned and how long the students have been exposed to it. On Fridays, I have a single-sided copy ready for students that I use as an assessment. I also have them track their progress and make a goal for the upcoming week. The goals are specific. For example, a student might choose 'subtracting 1/100 less from 1/10 less.' The following week, I have them review their goal quickly before diving into a new MathReps sheet.

Once a student has mastered a MathReps sheet, they are exempt from the daily practice and are given other tasks to do. They are still required to take the assessment on Fridays so that we can continue to monitor their mastery. There are times when modifications need to be made. Easy enough! Since the originals are digital, you can take out as many standards as a student needs to be successful.

Once most of the class understands the standards represented, I move on to the next set of standards. I then start the process all over again. I also throw in a week of an old MathReps to make sure they have retained the information. They are usually thrown off the first day, but then it all comes back.

Why it Works

It works because the students know what to expect every day. They understand how the paper looks. There is no navigating a new worksheet each day. It also works because students begin to see and make connections between methods. Again, looking at 5th grade, students start adding fractions using the area model and move to the standard algorithm. MathReps has them practicing both methods side by side daily. Students begin to see and understand the 'how' behind the methods.

Another reason MathReps work is simple; the more you practice something, the better you get. It's getting enough practice that muscle memory becomes automatic. Looking at the example of adding/subtracting decimals, my students had built enough muscle memory that they no longer needed to think about the process. This then clears the way for students to focus on solving the questions/tasks rather than struggle with how to solve problems and then tackle the calculations (remembering what to do with decimals).

Adaptations

As I've stated, creating individualized MathReps for students is easy. Some students may need fewer standards to practice. A few years ago, I had an eager student with an IEP in math. No matter how hard he tried, he struggled with the 8-12 standards. By working with his support teacher, we created a sheet that worked for him. It allowed him to practice on no more than five standards. No one in the class was aware that his MathRep was modified.

Assigning through an LMS or tools such as Google Classroom allow you to individualize the task efficiently. This further enhances a student's understanding and success.

Primary learners may need manipulatives to accompany Math-

Reps. A teacher can copy and place pacers in a clear plastic sleeve and use them as a math mat. Using a dry erase marker on the math mat will allow for easy cleaning. The teacher may have students use discs to place in the 10-frame and explore with connecting blocks to create number bonds (fact families).

Learn More

Explore more at:

- Mathreps.com
- Twitter #MathReps
- MathReps Facebook Group: bit.ly/MathRepsFBgroup
- MathReps Facebook Page: www.facebook.com/MathReps
- Contribute: bit.ly/MathRepsContribute

LISA M. NOWAKOWSKI

Lisa M. Nowakowski

Lisa is a Google Certified Innovator, Google Education Trainer, Google Innovator Mentor, PBS LearningMedia Digital Innovator, and presenter. She has helped others through her blog: NowaTechie.com. In 2010 Lisa was awarded the Crystal Apple Award sponsored by the local NBC affiliate. In 2015, she was Teacher of the Year at King City Arts Magnet. She has been an Ed Tech innovator in her district for over 20 years. After 25 years as a classroom teacher, she has transitioned into a Tech TOSA to further assist teachers in integrating technology in their classrooms. As a district technology leader, Lisa pioneered 1:1 Chromebooks in her district. Most recently, she has launched a podcast with Nancy Minicozzi (@coffeenancy) called - T.L.C. - Tech. Learn. Coffee that can be heard the first and third Monday of every month where ever you listen to podcasts. Creator and curator of MathReps.com - a free math resource to help students master math skills and find lasting success. This collection is available because of a collective effort among like-minded teachers who have been inspired by the EduProtocol Mindset. MathReps are available on several digital platforms.

19

2020 VISION OF DIGITAL CITIZENSHIP

MELISSA TORRENCE

> Vision without action is merely a dream. Action without vision just passes the time. Vision with action can change the world."
>
> — JOEL A. BARKER

The COVID-19 pandemic accelerated the amount of technology utilized by K-12 students, teachers, administrators, and parents for educational purposes across the globe. Digital citizenship and the ideas behind it are not new; however; in an all-virtual educational world, the importance of understanding online normalities was magnified. Implementation of digital citizenship in many educational institutions that I have been a part of has consisted of a section of time during one day, one week, or until a competition for designing a digital citizenship project/poster was complete. Sometimes the extent of information was the intentional delivery in the student/staff handbook and Acceptable Use Policy (AUP) paper that was reviewed at the beginning of the year and never mentioned again. Due to the lack of proactive conversations and ongoing, consistent lessons surrounding this topic, I have found that many educational stakeholders are not prepared to be a good digital citizen, even if their intentions are good. Unfortunately, people have not had exposure to these virtual expectations or how to enhance their brand until recent events, and now it is needed more than ever. I could have easily put on my glasses, watched the story unfold from the sideline without breaking a sweat. Instead, I decided to use my vision to change the level of exposure our community had to the virtual world, reduce fear surrounding technology use and give ideas and tips on building a positive virtual brand consistently and collaboratively.

Hindsight is 20/20

My first realization that digital citizenship was a need for students was several years before COVID-19. I was an assistant principal for a large district that had just implemented 1:1 devices for students to utilize while at school. There were many great things that this district did with inventory, educating teachers and students on how to utilize programs, ongoing support and training, providing campus technology instructional leaders, creating positive branding on social media platforms, establishing a discipline plan for technology misuse and etc. One of the major missing components at the time was teaching ALL students how to be good digital citizens. There were opportunities for interested students to win a prize if they submitted a digital citizenship poster for a week during the school year, and there were opportunities for students to learn if they made a technology mistake severe enough to land them in an assistant principal's office. This is where I realized that, as the assistant principal, I was the first person in many cases to have a conversation with students about digital citizenship and its importance. I addressed the issues that were presented but wanted students and parents to know and understand that a good digital citizen contributes valuable content and media to the virtual world.

During the 2020 educational transition, I again witnessed the need to educate students about digital citizenship. When having conversations with teachers and parents about issues that they were experiencing this Spring and having first-hand experience with Google Meet classes, the students were literally making silly faces and noises at the camera during class, and negative media was created on the chat feature. Google Classroom comments were not on topic or were inappropriate as well. I saw teachers and parents start to pull away from technology utilization in education and knew that I needed to take action. In anticipation of my current district continuing the use of technology and online classrooms for the fall semester, I wanted to be proactive rather than reactive. I needed to focus on how to build a plan.

A Focused Plan

I knew I needed an intentional plan but wasn't sure how to approach getting started. I had many things to consider: students' age, ease, and time for teachers to implement, quality of resources, engaging lessons, consistency, scheduling, and many others. I did not want the plan to be without focus and become well-intentioned individuals teaching information and landing on completely different objectives. I wanted the focus on learning and not the teaching. So, I searched Google, and it provided some great information, but I needed to make it fit my campus and community. I decided that I would need to start with a designated time for our educators to fulfill this task on my campus. Luckily it was already built into the schedule.

Scheduling/Intentional Lessons

The administrators on my campus had decided early summer to purposely build in additional time to the schedule for teachers and students to get the information or resources they needed to be successful. We anticipated stress to be high and that teachers would need additional time to communicate with parents. In addition to a tutorial period, we provided a "What I Need" (W.I.N.) time for twenty minutes every day. On Thursdays (which we changed to Tuesdays to better accommodate our staff), teachers would deliver a digital citizenship lesson to students during the W.I.N. time frame. We didn't want to add an additional task to their overloaded basket. To avoid that, I utilized the curriculums that I had found on Google and tailored them to our campus. Every week in our staff Google Classroom I shared lessons that consisted of Google slides, resources, teacher notes for each slide, and parent activity information for digital citizenship. Teachers could easily make a copy of the lesson and place it in their own Google Classroom for at-home learners and the students within their physical classroom. They had everything provided to them, and they could learn with their students.

Mapping the Details

Although teachers had lessons that were created for them, and all they had to do was share the information provided, there needed to be a flow and chunking of material. It was also important that the lessons I shared with teachers involved student-to-student conversations and that it wasn't information just being told to the students in a sit-and-get fashion. I wanted to incorporate student engagement within the slides with PearDeck or Nearpod, but this was challenging at the Intermediate (4th & 5th) level with limited tech hardware. We did not have devices for every student, and most students did not bring devices to school. PearDeck or Nearpod would have been great digital resources for engagement during the presentation if we had more devices.

Instead, I utilized Google Slides that took the class through guided whole-class conversations and activities. There were added presenter notes on the slides, and I also created a Google Doc with information and script for each slide, in case the teacher felt more comfortable with a printed copy. Students discussed with one another, wrote and drew on their desks with dry-erase markers, and then, after learning through a whole unit of digital citizenship, got to play an online game as a class to earn a badge. I printed and laminated badges for every student so that the teacher could give them out after the whole-group game. Students at home could also participate by saving their badge after completing that section of the game. Each unit had digital citizenship vocabulary that would be utilized throughout the unit, and it was reviewed each week before the lesson. Students were encouraged to use the vocabulary as they had conversations with classmates and shared their answers in class. The lessons were broken down into different units, which I got from the Be Internet Awesome (BIA) Curriculum. I edited and supplemented the BIA curriculum to what our community needed with Common Sense Education digital citizenship lessons too. The students on my campus were not the only individuals I wanted to reach. I wanted to provide information and assistance to their parents and other community members as well.

Parent and Community Involvement

Students' parents would receive activities and tips to help with digital citizenship for each unit. I shared this information through their homeroom Google Classroom, an email in Skyward, and some teachers sent it in the Remind App. After our campus completed the first unit, I met with many businesses within the community to place a

QR code in their place of business so that parents/community members could gain access to digital citizenship resources and learn with us. The post office, our grocery store, the hardware store, a few gas stations, churches, the donut shop, nail salons, restaurants, daycare facilities, and the police station posted this information. I also utilized Facebook and Twitter. Our administrative team also placed the community expectation for sharing digital citizenship into our campus improvement plan. More often than not, parents were excited about growing the citizenship side of their digital natives. Due to the campus sharing information, the fear of technology slowly started to subside in many areas.

In recent years there has been a push, especially in education, to educate individuals on citizenship in the digital world. The growing need for technology to assist in remediating or enhancing content during school is a huge factor. Society sets the norms on what a good digital citizen will possess. "This kind of change is everywhere in the workforce. However, change being advanced in our district isn't just about the workforce. It's also about how humans search, connect, communicate, and create as members of a global community, and within our own families. It's about citizenship, including digital citizenship" (Sheniger, 2014, p. 29).

Graphic courtesy of James "Carter" Torrence

Custom Frames

It is challenging and a little scary to build a "custom frame" for the community because you want the information to be the right fit and for them to understand the importance. Remember that custom frames still need adjustments from time-to-time.

 One of the most validating moments that I had this school year that helped me rest assured that I was moving in the right direction was right before the first lesson was taught in my school. A teacher stopped me in the hall to discuss what she had seen on a student device when helping the student set up an educational account. It was a sexually explicit website link. The teacher's first concern was that the student had searched and viewed the content at school. I pulled the student from class to ask a few questions and gain better insight into the concern. After speaking with the student, it was obvious that we also needed to commit time to digital safety and incorporate it into the citizenship lessons. The student said they had searched the website but not at school and had received the website link from an online stranger. The stranger had been playing an online video game earlier in the week. I asked the student why they would listen to a stranger, and the student stated, "They dared me to, so I did it." When I shared this information with the guardian, they were alarmed and embarrassed. In my conversation with the parent, I assured them that it was great to be alarmed because this was concerning. Still, they should not be embarrassed because we could work together to ensure the student learned about digital citizenship. I guided the parent to the proper Google Classroom and provided them with materials to use at home to grow a great digital citizen.

Digital Citizenship Curriculum Choices

There are many resources available to educators to address digital citizenship at their school. Be brave and tailor the curriculums to what your school needs. Be realistic about the level of digital citizenship at which your campus practices and what you want to accomplish by implementing this information. If you can address and support the appropriate level, it will make locating and/or crafting a curriculum much easier. Every school is different, and that is okay. The most important thing is that we grow and become better together.

- Be Internet Awesome Curriculum https://beinternetawesome.withgoogle.com/en_us/educators
- Common Sense Education https://www.commonsense.org/education/digital-citizenship/curriculum
- DigCitKids http://www.digcitinstitute.com/digcitkids.html

Suggestions

Without a plan for digital citizenship, schools will not be prepared for the many challenges that get in the way. There will be challenges. Keep moving forward.

Cover the "Do Not" List

In education, we often focus on the "Do Not" list rather than explaining to stakeholders what can be done. In all fairness, knowing the "Do Not" list is beneficial because it allows us to focus on what we should be doing, but we must be careful not to tarry in this area. This list could limit student creativity and learning.

It is similar to visiting the eye doctor and having a vision test. You learn what you can't see during the examination, but it is important to focus on what you can see after your sight has been corrected. If the eye doctor only told you what you couldn't see, you would miss out on many beautiful sights. It is easy to focus only on the negative side of digital citizenship and what we should not do as a digital citizen. Although it must be taught and understood, move forward to know what is available to digital citizens.

Emphasize the "Do" List

Although our intentions are good, we often miss the opportunity to share with students and other educational stakeholders what they should "do" as a good digital citizen and how it can enhance their opportunities. If we view the "Do Not" list and flip those ideas into a "Do" list, it makes a difference and supports the online journey (Cooksey, 2019). Students need to know that it is okay to advocate and brand themselves. Post-secondary institutions and employers will search for an individual and their digital footprint. If we are educating our students to create a digital path that shows all of the great steps they have taken, then we are guiding good digital citizens. The path doesn't have to be perfect but needs to lead in the right direction.

Conclusion

To grow good digital citizens, you can start small. It can be in your class, with a group of teachers or your school. Our students are digital natives and need guidance to become better digital citizens. Sometimes educators that are digital immigrants need guidance too. My current district has been great at setting the expectation to incorporate digital citizenship and let the campus decide how we would implement the information. Educating students on how to become a good digital citizen is just as important as teaching them how to become a good citizen in the physical world. Really, they are one and the same. I hope my experiences provide insight into building effective digital citizenship lessons that focus on growing and learning.

References

Be Internet Awesome. Digital Safety Resource. Retrieved July 21, 2020, from https://beinternetawesome.withgoogle.com/en_us/educators

Common Sense Education. Digital Citizenship Curriculum. Retrieved July 21, 2020, from https://www.commonsense.org/education/digital-citizenship/curriculum

Cooksey, A. Digital Citizenship: More Dos, Less Don'ts. Retrieved on August, 30, 2020 from https://knowledgequest.aasl.org/digital-citizenship-more-dos-less-donts/

Nearpod. Retrieved on 09/18/2020, https://nearpod.com/

Peardeck. Retrieved on 09/18/2020, https://www.peardeck.com/googleslides

Sheninger, E. (2014). Digital Leadership: Changing Paradigms for Changing Times. Thousand Oaks, CA: Corwin.

The Digital Citizenship Institute. DigCitKids. Retrieved September 7, 2020, from http://www.digcitinstitute.com/digcitkids.html

Torrence, J.C. (2020). Graphic Contribution.

Melissa Torrence

Melissa Torrence is a transformational leader, serving as an assistant principal in Hallsville, Texas. She has been a Solution Tree Press book reviewer for Dean Shareski's book *Embracing a Culture of Joy* and has been a photograph contributor to Laura Fleming's book *The Kickstart Guide to Making Great Makerspaces*. She is also a multiple time Texas Computer Education Association (TCEA) presenter and was recognized as a "VIP presenter" in 2020. She has been selected to present, Digital Citizenship: From Elementary to Community and pilot the Google Classroom for Administrators: Lead by Example workshop at the 2021 TCEA conference.

Melissa's experiences in education range from 1A (104.9 students and below) to 6A (2200 and above) districts, rural east Texas to the DFW metroplex and fourth through twelfth grades. She has served as a high school science teacher, UIL coordinator, instructional technology coach, middle school assistant principal and intermediate assistant principal.

Melissa and her husband, Jim, live in Hallsville, Texas and have two sons, Carter and Dalton. She loves watching her boys swim, ride their bikes and dig holes in the back yard.

She also enjoys connecting and growing with her Professional Learning Community. Reach out to her via Twitter @MelissaTorrence

20

COACHING WITH CLASS

STEPHANIE D. JACOBS

Explore coaching tips from the perspective of an instructional technology coach.

Before we jump into this chapter, can we establish something? I really want this to be an interactive chapter. What does that mean? I want this to be an opportunity for us to learn and grow together. As you are reading, trying out some new coaching strategies, some new instructional strategies, or some new technology tools, please reach out and share. You can share a tweet to @MsClassNSession, or use the hashtag #MsClassNSession on other social media platforms. In addition, we have a Voxer group specifically for technology coaches. If you want to join, feel free to drop me a line through email: msclassnsession@gmail.com. I look forward to our digital collaboration.

Introduction

Everyone has a story to tell and a path that they have taken to get to where they are professionally. In my years as an Instructional Coach, I have learned that there are many tips and tricks. The more we share with each other, the more we discover. My challenge for you is to take time and reflect on how you are using your journey to make a difference. This chapter will focus on instructional coaching in education. Take time to view the contents as a coach, as an administrator, and as a teacher. There are experts all around you. Sometimes the opportunity to share may be just what is needed to help you find your voice in this age of education advocacy.

My educational journey has been an amazing adventure lasting over twenty years. In my career, I have had the privilege of teaching in elementary classrooms ranging from preK to fifth grade, a variety of socio-economic communities (but mostly Title I), and even part-time as a college instructor. For a short time, I was a building principal and all of that has benefited me in my current role as an Instructional Technology Coach.

What is Coaching?

As an Instructional Coach (IC), it can sometimes be difficult to explain your role to those outside of education. As an IC, it can sometimes be difficult to explain your role to those working IN education. Coaching is a fairly new concept in many schools/districts. For that reason, it can be a little hard to accept. Successful coaching exists in an environment and culture of true collaboration. Each educator is looking to build their capacity for supporting student growth. Coaches exist for various areas: math, literacy, and technology, to name a few. In my experience, the role of a technology coach can be confused with that of a technician. While many technology coaches can assist with troubleshooting devices, programs, and software, I believe their main focus is supporting authentic technology integration in the classroom.

(Photo credit: Vanessa Jacobs)

This will be my fourth year as an Instructional Technology Coach, and each year I grow and learn a little more. My approach each year is a little different as well. Most will tell you that an important step to coaching is building relationships. This is an ongoing process. There are numerous ways that you can build relationships with your colleagues. For example, spending time talking and getting to know each other. Maybe you set up snack stations for those hectic days. Or you could help out in areas that may seem outside of the norm (read aloud to the class, give the teacher a bathroom break, make copies, etc.). Find something that works best for your situation, or try them all! In some areas and/or schools, you might find that traffic in and out of your school is constant with new staff starting and some leaving for other destinations. If this is the case, you may be introducing your role to new teachers every year. A benefit here is that you can always reinvent yourself until you find the best version (or the version you like best). But, it is also important to note that building relationships will be an ongoing component of coaching. In this chapter, I will share eight coaching tips that I think will be invaluable to your successful journey in coaching. You will find in these tips that you are ultimately the one in the driver's seat.

*Coaching Tips
from MsClassNSession*

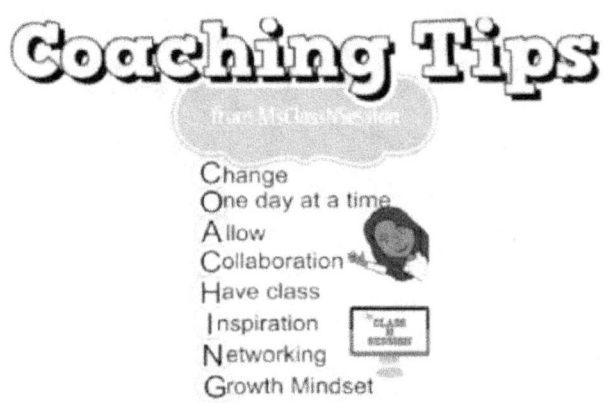

Tip #1: Change. I'm not sure why change causes such anxiety for us. Of course, it happens to me too. If I can hold on to my old, usual way, I most certainly will. But change is inevitable! We learn, we grow. Some things become obsolete. We experience change all the time in our lives. Each day is a new day to experience change. As we get older, we do things differently. Change happens. The best thing to do is embrace it. How can opportunities for change make us better?

In the role of IC, your mission is to support and encourage change with instruction. One thing that I love about technology is that it gives you a natural vehicle to try something new. It could be a new website, a new tech toy, or some other software development that can enhance your approach to instruction. Growth is constant. Sometimes, you just find a new way to use an old favorite. In the world of technology, this type of change is often intimidating. The main goals are to start slow, build on what you know, and make it your own. It's impossible to learn everything. Even when you think you have learned as much as you can, you find out there's more. So don't sweat the small stuff and when you learn a new way to do something...celebrate!

Tip #2: One day at a time. Who else has a tendency to take on too much? I do. I must constantly remind myself to breathe. One of the things that I love about my smartwatch is that it is constantly reminding me to breathe. So I take it slow. Take small steps. Take it one day at a time. As an IC, you help teachers to focus on the things within their control. That is true more often than not with technology. I know we have all experienced those technology fails. The internet is down, pesky printer issues, the copier is jammed (AGAIN!); these are just a few examples. It's okay. Tomorrow will be a better day. And guess what. They will work again!

Speaking of "one day at a time,"...what has been successful for you with scheduling coaching cycles/sessions? I must admit that I have struggled to find something that I love or that really works for me. If you are a technology coach, you probably balance your time between instruction and troubleshooting. And let's be honest, sometimes troubleshooting can just take over. You become the technician instead of the coach. As an IC, you must establish two things: 1) Your scheduling options and 2) Your coaching procedures. Of course, there is room for flexibility. But for your sanity, you definitely want to establish a system and routine. In the past, I have tried using the tool "YouCanBookMe." The problem for me was that someone would book me to teach a lesson 10 minutes from NOW, based on my calendar availability. Make it clear that this booked time is for a one-on-one session. It will be time to plan, and together, you will determine when modeling, observations, team teaching, etc., will occur. Coaches are just like teachers (we are teachers). We still need time to plan, time to gather resources, time to check in with you to determine your exact goal for the lesson. Last year, I worked consistently with several teachers, and our plan of action included the following: a pre-conference session--some time to sit down and establish goals. A "you do it" approach allowed the teacher to implement the strategy or specific tech tool. And finally, some follow-up, feedback, and/or reflection. I think by nature, teachers are reflective in their practice. As a coach, I like being able to listen to teachers work through the process of discovering what works, what needs a little more tweaking, and what can just be thrown right out the window. Sometimes you will do things on the fly, and that's okay, but I would not suggest living in a world of constant chaos and putting out fires. Develop a system that works for you and your staff. Allow this to be a work in progress if needed.

Tip #3: Allow. You are still in control even when you feel out of control. Allow yourself to live. Allow yourself to make mistakes. Allow yourself to explore and take risks. The best way to encourage and support our students (or even each other) is by sharing our own experiences. So we must give ourselves permission to have those experiences.

I must warn you here that I am one of those older educators. You know the kind. In today's curriculum, there are so many mandates and must-do's, but I am ultimately going to do what's best for students. For some teachers, this is scary. I hear all the time, "I'm a rule follower." Don't get me wrong, I like rules too. Structure and rules are my friends. But, the main rule that I follow is to get out of the way of student growth. I believe that we must allow our students to be great. One of my latest loves is coding with students. When I was in the classroom, my students would learn to code and then teach others to code. Their audiences ranged from other first graders to high school students to other adults (including our superintendent and one of our state senators). With coding, I love to see students' minds at work, the productive struggle of trying to make it all work, and finally, the creativity of a finished product. Recently, I worked with a teacher who wanted her ESOL (English to Speakers of Other Languages) students to use coding to practice their use of English in various ways. They created coding stories. There was one student who did not speak English, but she created a very detailed story through coding. It was also inspiring to see the other students work with her to assist with the final product. Imagine the opportunity that could have been missed if we did not allow ourselves to try something new, if we did not allow the students to work together, or if we did not allow the students to be creators of content. I applaud the teacher for stepping out of her comfort zone and normal lesson plan. I applaud the students for stepping into something new with such enthusiasm and a true spirit of collaboration.

Tip #4: Collaboration. I have been in education for over twenty years. I remember those days when I just wanted to close my door and do my own thing. My viewpoint changed during my time as an administrator. When I could go from classroom to classroom and see the wonderful teaching happening around me, I felt cheated. It was at that point that I began to see the light. When I went back into the classroom, my focus was different. It wasn't about me and what I felt comfortable with doing. It truly became about what was best for students. And for that reason, I stepped outside of my comfort zone. I have never regretted it.

This is important: True collaboration means working together. In education, that can be hard. In working together, we must give a little of ourselves, and we each must give in a little. Sometimes our tightly held beliefs will need to change. Recently, in a meeting of coaches, we had to prioritize the following three words: Practices, Resources, and Beliefs. How do you rank these three? When working together with the IC, all three are important, and how you prioritize them may shift from session to session. I think the beauty in collaboration is that you allow that shift to happen.

Recently, I was named as a SCASD Emerging Leader. For me, this is the ultimate opportunity for collaboration. Our cohort consists of educators with a variety of experiences. We are coaches, administrators, professors, and even education business leaders. Is your mind blown right now? Can you just imagine the work that will come from this group? Our overarching focus is on educating the whole child, so as I work with staff in our building, I am constantly thinking of not just technology, but how the work we do will serve and benefit the whole child. That leads to more collaboration opportunities among staff, students, other professionals, our administration team, and parents. It becomes a continuous cycle of working together and creating greatness.

Tip #5: Have CLASS. This is my favorite tip. And as an IC, it may be the one you lean into the most. Coaching is hard work. Even though you may host classes for professional development, you will need a dose of CLASS when dealing with any negative energy. There may be initiatives that won't be met with open arms. Brace yourself. Keep a positive attitude and move forward anyway.

Now, don't get me wrong. Having CLASS doesn't mean that there won't be bad days. You will have moments of weakness. After all, having CLASS also means giving yourself (and others) the grace to simply be human. I know that in the world of technology, everyone does not share my same love, passion, or my attitude to Just Try IT! I wasn't always this techie person who sits before you today. Each and every day, I am still in class. I continue to learn new things. I continue to grow. I am a student of technology, and attending conferences allows me to connect with other like-minded professionals and experts in the field. I share many strategies and resources. I share them with the understanding that some of those ideas will spark interest, and others will hit the floor with a resounding...THUD.

Tip #6: Inspiration. As an educator, sometimes it can be difficult to find your muse. That thing (or person) that inspires you. When I became an IC, it wasn't the career path that I was seeking. But I am thankful that I took a chance on it. Though I find inspiration in many ways, I am most inspired by students. Listening to their goals, their dreams, and seeing their creativity come to life are examples of the inspirations they provide. As an IC, you may be an inspiration to those you serve, but also take advantage of opportunities to find inspiration from those around you.

Okay, so I really don't want to name drop here, BUT... I will! I find inspiration among my colleagues as well. The power of social media is that you can have a strong connection to people whom you have never met. Then that leads to opportunities to attend conferences and workshops where you do get the chance to come face-to-face with someone who has inspired you from behind a screen or monitor. I will say that I am mostly inspired by some everyday, down-to-earth people—people who give you the feeling that a conversation with them is completely effortless. And many are from my great state of South Carolina. The work and accomplishments of Carla Jefferson (Instructional Technology Coordinator) and Chanda Jefferson (former SC Teacher of the Year)---not sure if there is any relation--- reminds me to keep pushing to be my best self. I can be from a little small town in South Carolina and still achieve great things. Even if my work never leaves the walls of my school or the borders of my county, I know that I have made a difference at some point in some child's life, in some teacher's life. And that truly is enough. Next up is my colleague, and I like to call him my dear friend--Jed Dearybury (Educator, Author, Illustrator). When I think about Jed, I think about fun times. He is all about the power of play in the classroom. Not only did he write a book about it, but he truly embodies that in real life. There is never a dull moment when working with Jed. You will tap into the depths of your imagination—imagination, the sacred place that we want all students to forever hold on to in their endeavors. I am trying to keep my list short, but I must mention my IC muse--Matt Miller. He is the author of the Ditch That Textbook series and hosts the phenomenal Ditch Summit every year.

Although I am new to Ditch Summit, these are the resources that I consistently share with teachers and staff. I recently completed Matt Miller's Remote 101 online course, and it was worth every minute! Also, I was inspired to start creating my own infographics.

Last but not least is my leadership inspiration, Principal Baruti Kafele. During the pandemic of 2020, he has been generously committed to presenting a FREE Virtual Leadership Academy. At the point of writing this chapter, I have faithfully attended every session on Saturday morning. The academy is intended for aspiring assistant principals, but the content is relevant to anyone in a leadership capacity. Principal Kafele challenges your thinking with a series of questions that urge you to reflect on your practice. I am sure that many of these are not the usual names you see in the "educelebs" conversations. As I mentioned in my introduction: experts are all around you. You may even find one right in your building!

Tip #7: Networking. I love the idea of breaking down the walls of education. Expanding your network will allow you to do that. In my coaching and professional circles, I enjoy making connections outside of the building where I work. Those networks expose me to new ideas and ways of thinking that I may not find in my day-to-day interactions. Then, as an IC, I can bring those new ideas back to share.

How can I write this chapter without including a "Hamilton" reference? This musical has been the single most influential thing in my life during the pandemic and days of quarantine. And so, let this reverberate in the background of this section, "I am not throwing away my shot." That famous line is the foundation of networking: find your opportunity and take advantage of your shot. When I am working with teachers, I often advocate for the power of social media. Some may view it as a vice, but I believe it is all in how you set up your network, your professional learning network. It's okay to be discerning about who you connect with and how you build your own social media footprint. This section is an extension of the previous one. Each one of the educators that I mention is a part of my professional network. Some I have met, and some I have only communicated with through social media. Still, I consider my network to be filled with distinguished, dedicated professionals. And I am proud to know each one of them. Also, two groups that I am proud to include in my circle are SC for Ed and SCASCD Emerging Leaders. Both organizations/groups provide me with a platform to advocate for education, educators, and students. In our nation's current climate, this is extremely important. When people say, "Use your teacher voice," it not only applies to your time in the classroom but also applies to relevant educational issues that require teachers/educators to speak up on their own behalf. That expert in your building is YOU. You know the profession, you know the needs of students, you know what works, you know what has flopped. Advocate for what is right. Advocate for what our students deserve. High-quality education in every school, for every student. **Drops the mic, steps off soapbox, ends this section**

Tip #8: Growth Mindset. If you are in the role of coaching, you probably have demonstrated a growth mindset. Successful coaching requires an awareness that you are not expected to know it all. You just have a willingness to try new things. To research new ideas. A willingness to do the work.

Let me finish with my personal growth mindset story and hopefully you can find inspiration in it, especially if you are ever a little hesitant to try something new. Before beginning my coaching journey, I became a risk-taker in the classroom. I quickly learned that this was exactly what my students needed to excel. They exceeded my expectations by leaps and bounds. And their growth mindset inspired me to develop my skills in technology which would soon benefit me in my new role as Instructional Technology Coach. I took a chance and enrolled in a course/summer camp to explore skills and techniques in the area(s) of computer science, coding, cybersecurity, ethical hacking, etc. Some pretty heavy stuff! Talk about intimidation, but I was willing to learn. In the end, I successfully completed the course feeling like a cyber expert. I would go on to present at a conference with the site coordinator. Trust me, I know that it can be hard to step out into the unknown. This is one of the many reasons that I am passionate about developing a growth mindset in students and in teachers. You have the ability to reach beyond your limitations if you just take a giant leap of faith!

Coaching in a Pandemic

I began writing this chapter in 2019, but I am grateful to have a chance to revisit it. Things have certainly changed. The world has changed. Now I will have the added experience of coaching in a pandemic. In March of 2020, our lives changed as we stopped what we were doing, ended our school year months early, and faced the challenge of dealing with COVID-19.

When we look back on 2020, I wonder if we'll ask ourselves, "How did we make it through?" So much has changed in education, in our lives. Everyone is being called on to learn new ways of doing things and to use tools and strategies that we may not have used before (or maybe just at a different level). In the midst of it all, coaching has its own challenges. How do we find balance in the wake of so much change? Yes, we want to support teachers, but at the same time, we don't want to apply too much pressure. Everything is so fragile right now—the internet, our emotions, and maybe sometimes even our patience. The words that you will hear uttered often in the hallways of schools are grace and flexibility. We must extend this to others, and at the same time, we must give ourselves permission to feel what we are feeling and give ourselves some much-needed grace.

In my district, we are trying different things with coaching in the area of technology. One of them is called "on-demand lessons." The premise is to present professional development information, tips, and resources in short 4 slide presentations. Of course, another creative tool that is sweeping education is the Bitmoji classroom. If you have been anywhere near a classroom or school, I'm sure you have seen at least one of these creations. Caution to educators: these fun, interactive inventions can consume hours of your time. But then again, that can be a great stress reliever as you work at building the ultimate online classroom or office space. In my role as an IC, I have enjoyed creating templates for teachers to use in the ways they see fit. I have also created my own templates for sharing information with staff.

What's Next: A Technology Challenge

As we bring this chapter to a close, I would like to leave you with a little technology challenge. Remember, this should be an interactive chapter. So, here is your final chance to interact with other educators. Take a few minutes to share the coaching tip that resonated the most with you using this Flipgrid code: 6e972280

As an added incentive, once we get to 10 unique responses, there will be a drawing for a $25 TPT (Teachers Pay Teachers) or Amazon gift code. A second code will be drawn if/when we reach 25 unique responses. Finally, if/when we get to the grand number of 50 unique responses, there will be a final drawing for a TPT/Amazon gift code.

Happy sharing!

Stephanie D. Jacobs

Stephanie D. Jacobs is a veteran with over 20 years in education. Stephanie resides in beautiful Rock Hill, SC, and is currently an Instructional Technology Coach. Her background includes teaching in grades PreK-5, as well as serving as an elementary school principal and adjunct Reading instructor. Stephanie has also been recognized as a SCASCD Emerging Leader and works with the teacher advocate group SC for Ed as an Area Representative. She is passionate about education and shares her passion through blogging and presenting at a variety of educational conferences. Let's connect!
Twitter: https://twitter.com/msclassnsession
Blog: https://msclassnsession.weebly.com/this-blog-is-why
Website: www.msclassnsession.weebly.com

21

EDUCATIONAL BLACKSMITHING

MELINDA VANDEVORT

I have a friend that is a modern-day blacksmith. He creates beautiful works of art with metal. The forging process starts with metals that are full of dross, something that is trivial or inferior. He refines the metal by heating it until it has all the characteristics he is looking for in the end product, and those things that don't add value are refined until they are no longer present. Professional learning is the process of refining those desirable skills in teachers until they are beautiful works of art. There are different types of refining because not all metals are the same, and they need to be refined differently to produce the intended outcome. Teacher learning should be the same, personalizing and "refining'"; the learning based on the teacher's needs and intended outcome.

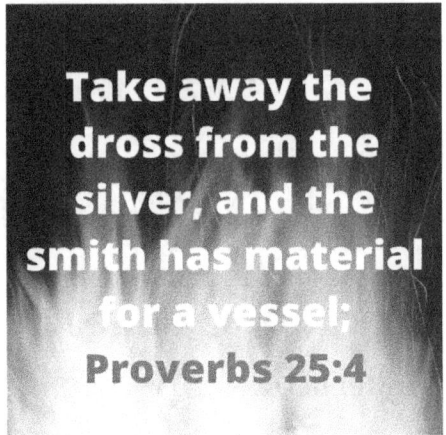

Traditionalized or Personalized?

Professional development (PD) is a term that evokes an array of emotions in teachers, from excitement to dread. If we change up the terminology and create a way to empower teacher learning, then we can change the face of traditional professional development. Teachers learn to take control and ownership of their learning the same way that we encourage our students. Let's start with a name change. Instead of calling it professional development, which dons a negative connotation for some, let's call it professional learning. This brings a fresh and new sense to the word.

I won't say that I hate PD, quite the contrary. I love learning new things that inspire me to be better at my job and teach others how to do the same. I do, however, hate my time being wasted on things that are not relevant to me or shoved at me so fast I don't have time to process what I learned. One reason so many teachers dread PD is that somewhere along the way, it became that sit-and-get method of shoving information at teachers and assuming they were going to be "all the better" after it. Development is, by definition, creating growth, progress, or positive change. Professional development, in itself, is not a bad thing. Whole group PD can get you pumped up, inspired, and ready to tackle the year with enthusiasm. However, that enthusiasm isn't sustainable. I don't think development is the problem, we all want to develop our skills. I think delivery is the problem. Professional learning, on the other hand, has a more positive overtone, and teachers are more willing to embrace it.

Why does the term professional learning have a more positive effect on teachers? Why should we move toward this method of adult learning? Learning insinuates the on-going process of knowledge acquired through experience. Teachers need to experience their learning in basically the same way students experience theirs. Teachers must be active participants in their learning, or it simply becomes knowledge acquisition without application. Teachers should always be in pursuit of more knowledge as the catalyst for teaching students. Methods change, tools are added, and teachers need to keep up to stay effective and increase student achievement to the max. It should be the mission of every administrator and every teacher to make sure that they are getting the personalized and targeted professional learning needed to fully develop their skills to best meet their students' needs.

Infusing personalized professional learning into a building starts with conversation—conversations between principals and teachers about strengths first, and then growth opportunities. Starting conversations with strengths empowers teachers and paves an open road for rich conversation about growth areas. Another reason to start with strengths is for principals to learn what their teachers are good at to leverage personal strengths for other professional learning opportunities. Professional learning must be sustainable, and for that to happen, it must be personal for the teacher receiving it.

As a principal, I needed to make sure that my teachers were getting what they needed and were interested in professionally. If a teacher is not a technology guru but wants or needs to be more effective in their teaching, technology is what they need to learn. What about that new teacher that hasn't mastered classroom management yet? They're assigned a mentor, and their learning focuses on that growth area. It's all about knowing what teachers need and are inspired by and offering learning tasks to ensure they can reach mastery.

Through a principal's lens, I could see what needed to be adjusted in each individual classroom and how to affect change by leveraging my human resources in the building. Through the lens of a consultant, I see how I can affect change on a broader scale. I can show educational leaders how to adopt this way of thinking and take professional learning to a whole other level. It is knowing how to personalize learning for each teacher that is the key to success. Is it harder this way? Yes, but it is leadership's job to ensure every teacher is getting what they need to succeed. It is not ok to ask teachers to personalize student learning so that every child can succeed if we aren't doing the same for our teachers. This is modeling at its best.

Mobilizing PPL

Personalized professional learning (PPL) should be targeted, sustainable, active, and applicable. Professional learning should be more than that sit-and-get method; it should be forward moving, mobile. What should PPL look like, then?

Consider these four things; it is:

- **Active:** Teachers are involved in creating their personal learning plans. Vested teachers are more likely to be independent learners when they are involved in the process.
- **Targeted:** Growth areas are the main focus of the learning plan. It is specific to the content area, based on teacher

growth areas from evaluation and conversation between teacher and principal.
- **Sustainable:** The learning is not a one-time event; there is practice, reflection time, and the feedback loop is closed through rich conversation for continued growth.
- **Applicable:** The learning is relevant, not only to the teacher's needs, but also to their interests. Teachers are inspired by what they are learning. It fits the grade level they teach.

> A teacher who is attempting to teach without inspiring the student to learn is like hammering on cold iron-
> Horace Mann

Adult learners are no different than student learners in a lot of aspects. If I am not interested in what I am learning or it isn't relevant to my needs, I am probably going to be a poor student of learning at that point. Give teachers a reason to be inspired and excited about their learning. When teachers are excited about their learning, that carries over into the classroom. Refining brings out the best of something, whether that something is metal or people.

References

Darling-Hammond, L., Hyler, M. E., Gardner,

M. (2017). *Effective Teacher Professional Development*. Palo Alto, CA: Learning Policy Institute.

Refining of Metals. (2010). Retrieved August 23, 2020, from https://encyclopedia2.thefreedictionary.com/Refining+of+Metals

Photos created with Canva

Educational Blacksmithing

Melinda Vandevort

Melinda (Mel) has been in education in one capacity or another for over 20 years in the Missouri school system. She has taught everything from preschool to high school and recently moved into administration. Mel is currently working on her doctorate degree in Educational Leadership in which her research is steeped in adult learning theory and using professional learning as a catalyst to increase student achievement. Mel has recently ventured into the world of podcasting as well. Her podcast, Empowered Educator, focuses on professional learning to empower educators to take control and ownership of their own professional learning. She is also venturing into consultancy to educate others with her knowledge of technology in the classroom and using technology as a professional learning platform. Mel is a Google Certified Educator, Wakelet Ambassador, Screencastify Genius and Edpuzzle Coach. When she is not focused on education, she is playing piano, gardening, or traveling with her family. You can connect with Mel @MelVandevort on Twitter, Instagram, and LinkedIn or catch her podcast on Spotify, Apple Podcasts, and Stitcher. Visit her website Empowered Educator at www.empowereducator.com.

22

A SPIN ON SERIOUS

REBECCA GIBBONEY

Day in and day out, everything seems so serious, but does it have to be? Take charge. Be the solution. Put a spin on serious with gamification in the workplace.

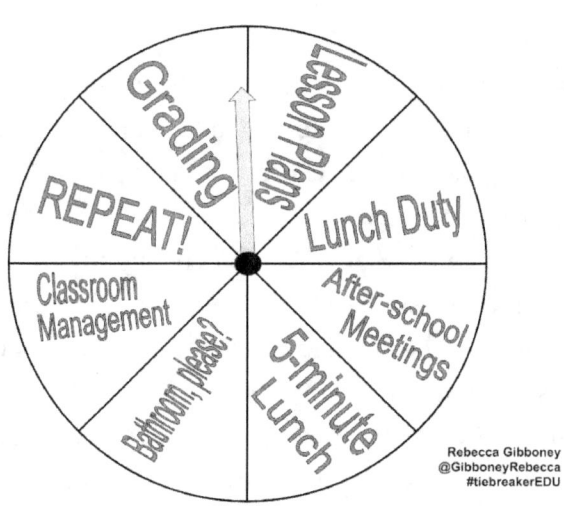

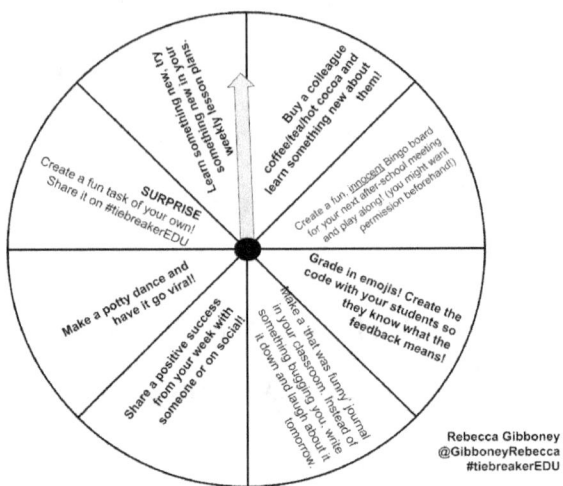

Rebecca Gibboney
@GibboneyRebecca
#tiebreakerEDU

Check, check plus, check, check minus. "Hmm, this student didn't even add their name!" For heaven's sake!

My lesson plans for today? Yes, a post-it will just need to do.

Untouched vegetables, five empty Scooter Crunch wrappers laying on the lunch tray. Meanwhile, let me walk through the rows of student cafeteria tables and scarf down my salad of leftover vegetables from my fridge.

Which after-school meeting do I have today? Let's check my Outlook calendar, my Google Calendar, and, oh yes, even my old school paper agenda. All because we cannot find a single method to streamline meeting invites.

"Señorita, are you okay? You're dancing kind of funny," asks my adorable, innocent estudiante. "¡Oh sí! This is just Señorita's baño dance because she hasn't had a chance to run to the bathroom yet today," ...as the clock strikes 2:00 pm.

"Please take out your ear pods, airbuds, earbuds...whatever you call them." "No, you cannot go to the baño; you just went." "What do you mean, you do not have a lápiz?" "Una respuesta, por favor." Crickets. "I have dulces." All shout out at once, no hands raised.

REPEAT!

This was me for 180 days, day in and day out, about five years ago. No matter the day, we could spin that wheel of fate, and one of those tasks was bound to exhaust me by the end of the day. Sure, I may have exaggerated a little bit, but this is the reality for teachers worldwide. We see it plastered on social media. We see it weighing down the bags under their eyes. Sadly, we see it as we continue to experience a teacher shortage. But why?

You may be in disbelief after reading those comments because you may never experience a teacher day like that. Kudos to you! On the contrary, you may live that wheel of fate and feel guilty that you are not doing enough.

Do not!

Instead, wipe the tears and stop looking in the mirror at the bags under your eyes. You are doing enough; you ARE enough! Most teachers experience these emotions, and if they don't, I would love to learn from them.

I can reflect now and admit that five years ago, I had reached the point of burnout--something I never thought I could experience until it hit me. I was unsure I could hit repeat one more day. I was unsure I could show up for my students one more day. I was just unsure about everything. Yet, I knew education was the place for me. My heart and mind were playing tug of war with my emotions.

I kept coming back to why? Why did I feel like I was hitting repeat? Why did it all feel so monotonous?

Why was it all so serious? That was it. It was all just too serious when it did not have to be. I was no longer having fun with what I was doing day in and day out; and, I was the only one that could fix it.

The Solution

I have always found myself as a solution-seeker. If there is a problem, I will find an answer. Maybe not today and maybe not tomorrow, but I'll find one with time. Five years ago, I knew that if I was playing this tug of war game, so were some of my colleagues. We needed to bring some fun into the workplace. We needed to put a spin on serious!

I spent some time trying gamification in my classroom with my students, and then it dawned on me...lightbulb moment...why can't we use gamification with adults? Who was there to say no? It was time to bring the fun to the workplace.

What I (We) Learned

As an Instructional Coach and classroom teacher, I did not have the authority to call all of the shots. However, I found that my principal was very supportive and a huge teammate when it came to this idea of adult gamification. It was nothing new. Yet, it is something that we never thought about to elevate our own game as professionals. As we started to put a spin on serious, we learned a thing or two (okay, maybe a few more) about ourselves and our staff.

- Not everyone plays the game, but everyone wants to play the game!

Not everyone jumps in and plays the game right away. They hesitate and question. Who wouldn't? It is something new, and with new comes change, and with change comes resistance. Yet, what we found was that everyone did want to play. We had to find a way to include everyone and make everyone feel some level of success. We never made these challenges mandatory. In fact, some of the challenges no one played! That was okay! The idea was that everyone had a chance.

- Instead of professional development, we embraced a culture of professional learning.

Every year we introduced new initiatives to our colleagues. New writing curriculum, socio-emotional learning, classroom assessments, state mandates, etc. The list goes on, and this cyclical pattern developed. We would introduce the new and improved initiatives, teachers would "implement" these ideas, and then the following year, they would get something new. Something we like to call in the world of education "initiative fatigue." There was no follow-through, no accountability, no reflection. As we started to roll out gamification challenges throughout the year, we were intentional about what types of tasks we included. Our tasks always included new ideas but also recycled old programs or initiatives that we have covered. Teachers started to see consistency and appreciate what they were learning.

- If the teachers are having fun, the students are having fun.

In our education world, the emphasis is always on the student, which, of course, it should! However, I believe we tend to focus so much on the students that we forget about the educators. Yes, we want our students to be achieving, having fun, and growing; but, how will our students be successful if our teachers aren't successful? One cannot be expected to fill someone else's cup when their cup is empty. We must fuel our educators so that they are empowered and energized enough to fuel our students. It was amazing to see how much our students started to play along with our gamification. Our teachers were having fun, and our students were having even more fun!

At first, my naive-self believed that I could just go with it and implement gamification tomorrow—spoiler alert. I was wrong! I should have known better. I should have listened, and I should have empathized. Therefore, it should not have come as a surprise when no one--and I mean no one--participated in my first gamification. Instead of hearing cheers, I heard laughs. Instead of high fives, I got open palms to the face. What was Becky having us do this time? And...they were right! In my book, The Tiebreaker, I go into detail about the Five Keys to Victory, what you need to think about before really diving into the implementation of gamification. What I wish I would have known then what I know now.

1. Invest and Value ALL of Your Staff
2. Drive Your Vision
3. Recruit Your Dream Team
4. Your X's and O's
5. The Regen Effect: Reward, Reflect, Refine

If I would have followed more of the above advice and the advice detailed in my book, I truly believe my gamification would have been more successful the first time around; but, isn't that what innovating is all about? Being graceful and asking for permission to get back up after a failure? To learn and try again? After a couple of practice runs, I finally figured it out, and we changed the game of professional learning for our colleagues.

Your Challenge

I challenge you to put a spin on serious. If you find yourself always being so serious, ask yourself why? Life, work, it does not always have to be so serious. We, ourselves, make it that way. Ask for permission to try something new. Grant yourself permission to fail and try again. No one deserves to feel how I felt five years ago. Yet, again, I found that I was my own worst enemy. Are you your own worst enemy? For me, gamification was my solution. For others, it might be something different. I challenge you to find your solution and be the solution.

Along the way, try gamification. Why not? It may just be your spin on serious.

Insert

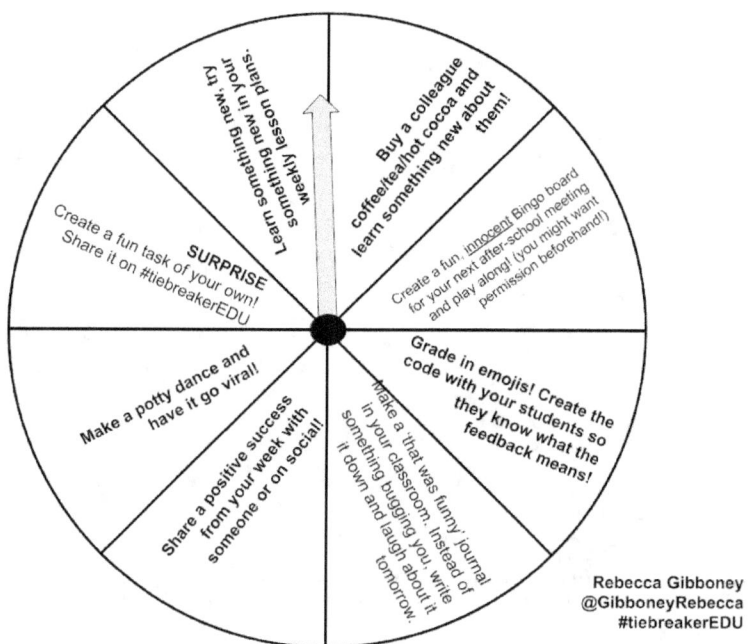

Gamification Example:

LTMS Tailgate Challenge

Are you ready to kickoff another amazing school year?!

In order to kickoff another school year, we will be competing in our LTMS Tailgate Challenge. Like in the past, grade-level teams will be competing against one another (mini-course and related arts teachers will be assigned a team and special education teachers will be with their grade level).

Purpose:
- Build community within our building
- Understand Bloom's Taxonomy and Webb's DOK
- Integrate critical verbs and Collin's Writing into Bloom's and Webb's

How does it work?
- Certain points will be allocated to each team when a team member makes a "big play" (aka completes a task).
- Points will be updated once the 'big plays' are reviewed
- Winning team gets a surprise!

How do I accumulate points for my team?

QUARTER 4

Fumble recovery – 1 point
- Complete a Collin's Writing (any Type)
- Integrate a critical verb in a question stem
- Complete a low level DOK (1 or 2) or Bloom's (remember/understand)
- Take a 'team picture' with your best 'game face'.

Safety – 2 points
- Use a new app or website in your classroom.
- Write someone (a student or coworker) a pep talk and make their day. This should be thought provoking and meaningful! Show your proof by emailing me (rleid@loyalsocklancers.org) the note with a signature of the person who received your talk. *Extra point: act out the pep talk and really dramatize it! Send the proof (a recording) of your performance to me!*
- Complete a DOK (3 or 4) or Bloom's (Apply, analyze, evaluate, create)

Field goal – 3 points

- Share with a colleague an activity how you integrated all three (Webb's or Bloom's, critical verbs, and Collins) that <u>you tried out in your classroom.</u> Discuss if it was a success or something you need to adjust for future use. Email me evidence!
- Choose an area of focus and invite a colleague to visit your classroom to give you feedback.
- Email me 3 ways you connected or learned something new about your students in your Lancer Period.
- Give your Lancer Period a pep talk

Touchdown – 7 points
- Invite the coach to come in and check out critical thinking in action.
- Reflect with a coach about creating questions and create an activity or worksheet for the classroom using questioning strategies.
- Develop a low-level question and scaffold the question to eventually complete a high level question
- Create a lesson that encourages critical thinking in your classroom. Share with a co-worker and then make copies for your colleagues!
- Make team shirts for a dress down day. Everyone must wear them!

Interception – 7 points and deduct 3 points from any team
Complete a full BDA with a coach.

If you are interested in hearing more about building a culture of gamification, check out Rebecca Gibboney's book, *The Tiebreaker,* on Amazon: https://bit.ly/theTIEBREAKER or visit her website: www.rebeccagibboney.com.

Rebecca Gibboney

Rebecca Gibboney is currently a Curriculum Specialist but started her career in education in 2010 as a Spanish teacher and Instructional Coach in Williamsport, Pennsylvania. She is passionate about two things in life: sports and education. As a women's assistant college basketball coach and a passionate educational change agent, she lives the best of both worlds. She continues to provide fun and engaging avenues for adult learning while challenging the traditional mindset of professional learning. There is no reason why professional learning experiences cannot add some fun to the workplace!

Connect with the Author
rebeccagibboney.com | @GibboneyRebecca | #tiebreakerEDU

23

JUGGLE THE STRUGGLE
THE CHOICE TO SERVE

ERIN B. KIGER

We are in a servant, not service, servant profession. We serve. We serve our students, we serve our parents, we serve the other teachers and leadership we work with. To serve is one of the greatest honors that someone can be called to. You don't just wake up one day and decide you want to serve; it is in your heart, deep down. And when that service yields the growth that we strive for, I feel like our hearts grow like the Grinch (although it was never small, to begin with).

I already knew all of this. I'm sure you already knew all of this too. I think, though, that over time I'd had an epiphany when it comes to who we serve. I collected stories this year from several professionals in the education field. And while each story was different, the focus was on how we #jugglethestruggleEDU. As I read through the pages, as I reflect back on the stories, and as I discuss feedback, I realize that another common thread is that the struggle comes from our intense desire to serve.

Serving has to be one of the noblest callings. It is hard, and it can be intense, but it is done from a place of love and caring. Now, I'm not defining it...I didn't Google it from Merriam Webster or even Urban Dictionary. I'm just sharing my understanding based on my faith and my heart and how I was raised. I also realize that I'm making some huge generalities. But I'm making these statements based on what I know of so many educators. If this doesn't apply to you, cool. Not worried about it. No judgment. But if it does apply to you, think about this, do you struggle because your desire to serve others (students, parents, colleagues) feels stronger than your desire to serve your own family?

Our desire to serve our education community will, at times, blind us to the fact that we need to serve our family too. Remember how I said serving comes from a place of love and caring. Who else do we love and care for more than our own family? And who else loves and cares for us more than our own family? It is OK to put your family first. As professionals, we are expected to work a very specific and dedicated number of hours per our contract. Couple that with the (either implicit or explicit depending on your contract) number of hours that you are expected to work outside of your designated contract time, and it feels like the only people we CAN serve are our students, families, and colleagues. By the time we get to our families, we're running on empty. Our families miss out, and so do we.

You are a human, and you are a servant, and you are an educator. That is an outstanding combination that somehow seems to allow you to love and care for more people and about more things than is sometimes humanly possible. But as you head into another day of struggles, remember do not feel guilty. Who you serve must be your choice. Do not feel guilty for choosing to serve your family over your students. Do not feel guilty for closing your computer and playing a game with your own children. Do not feel guilty for letting the grading go for another day to have dinner together as a family.

Serving comes from a place of love and caring. Serve the people...do not serve the job. I need to take my own advice, and I wonder if my story to #jugglethestruggleEDU will become a little easier.

Hello! My name is Erin Kiger. I have worked in education for 16 years. I have been an elementary classroom teacher, an instructional technology coach in K-12, and worked on professional development in higher ed.

I have earned an MEd in Ed Tech and an MA in Educational Leadership. My passion lies in ed tech and nothing is more exciting to me than working with teachers and inspiring them to be just as excited as I am about the potential that ed tech can bring into the lives of their students.

On a more personal level, I have an incredible husband, Tony, and our little blessing, Matthew. Both of these boys bring so much joy, laughter, and light into my life on a daily basis. I have an unhealthy obsession with Disney, I love old books because of the way they smell, and I will always pick the chocolate dessert. In the end, I'm always up for a new adventure, however that may look…a trip to the beach, a virtual tour of a dream vacation, a podcast with my colleagues Ashley and Joelle, a new job at an edtech company, publishing a book with EduMatch, or battling my nemesis, Corona, with hand sanitizer and Clorox wipes (I'll get you Corona!! *shakes fist). I'm excited and honored to be able to share this story.

24

BECOMING THE TEACHER I WAS MEANT TO BE

JESSICA REED, ED.S.

The journey from becoming a teacher's kid to a teacher.

I am a teacher's kid. I remember sitting in my mom's classroom during the beginning/ending of school and going from room to room to see what things I could take home. I grew up with my mom coming home with papers to grade, and then she would attend class to receive several degrees. All I thought she did was read stories and tell the kids how to do something. I always enjoyed having my mom at home during the summer and during school holidays. As I grew up, I knew that I wanted to do something with kids, but I did not want to be in the classroom. Teaching was not my original plan; I knew that I wanted to work with kids but was unsure of what that would look like in the future. When I went to the University of Kentucky, my major was going to be agricultural leadership because I wanted to be a 4-H Agent. I had the pleasure of being a Georgia 4-Her and experienced so many great things from camping to learning how to complete presentations. The college of agriculture was a completely different place than I expected it to be. In my first semester, I was sitting in Plant and Soil Science learning about the DNA of a corn seed, and I started to question who really needs to know that? That is when I started to reevaluate my career aspirations and decided that maybe agriculture was not the job for me. Although I did learn several cool random facts about the impact of the horse industry in Kentucky, it can make a great ice breaker at gatherings. I thought that I would become a teacher because that teaching seemed like the easiest thing to do in the world. My classes ranged from learning about the theory of physics to learning about how to teach math in a general education classroom setting. While I did have several education classes, I did participate in several English classes because of my English concentration for my major.

My student teaching assignment was a fourth-grade all-inclusive gifted classroom. It was such a cool experience because I came up with several different activities that really challenged me as a teacher but did not equal to the realities of the classroom. While experiencing a classroom that contains gifted children is a dream, it was not the best way to start my teaching career. I thought that I was going to be a good teacher because I was a teacher's kid and knew how to run a classroom, or at least I thought I knew how to. When I graduated from Kentucky, I had a BA in elementary education and had a job as a kindergarten teacher. I was excited to be in the classroom with my own class. After the first day in kindergarten, I realized I was unsure of how to actually run a classroom and realized that kindergarten was not meant for me. I sat on the couch and said out loud, "Kentucky did not teach me how to handle a classroom." I finished out the year, knowing that I may need some extra help in the classroom with my management style and knowing I was not meant for younger students. Over the next few years, I would hold several different positions and be in different locations for personal reasons. Some of the jobs I have had include being a fourth-grade teacher, special education teacher for

K-6, a paraprofessional at a high school, and working at a school for students with behavior disorders.

I always thought that I was going to be one of the really cutesy elementary teachers. You know, the kind that always had the cute decorations and fun activities, and always had the best well-behaved class. Life is funny when you really start to be in the classroom because I was not the cutest teacher. For the first year, I did try to be cutesy, but it just did not work out. As I continued into my education career, I always thought that I would be an elementary school teacher, never a middle school teacher. As a kid, I was very awkward during the middle school years. When I moved to Alabama, I had the chance to be a special education teacher at a middle school, and I loved every minute of it. I was surprised because I did not think that I was going to love this age range. Middle school kids are fun to be around (most days), and they still think that you are cool enough. There is never a dull day, especially in the last few years. The one thing I have learned about being with middle schoolers is that you have to stay consistent and maintain your standards. This has made me realize that my classroom management has changed, and it has become better with more experience. I try to explain to my students that I have high expectations for them academically and behaviorally. I do not let my students get away with everything, but I try to establish that connection to let them know I do care for them. I also expect their best every day. My classroom is the one place that I can control what happens for the most part, and I want my students to realize how loved they are and that this is a safe space.

We all know that being a teacher that every day can be a complete surprise; it is either a good surprise or a bad surprise. Being in middle school, there are so many different emotions that can happen to students in an eight hour day. Middle school, just like any position, has really forced me to reexamine how I teach and connect with students. It has made me a better teacher because I have gained confidence and understanding in my craft. I do think that I have my dream job at the current moment. I am a language arts resource teacher, which means I teach language arts to 6th, 7th, and 8th graders, but in a small group setting. I get to have the same kids every year. I get to try all sorts of different ideas that include technology and even creating slime for an informational piece of writing. I have learned that I love to teach Edgar Allan Poe and love being able to push my students to think beyond watching Tik Toks. Most days, I love what I am teaching, even if my kids want to complain about different writing assignments. It is crazy to think that I get paid to do this and get to see some of the coolest kids I have ever known.

I always knew I loved my kids, but the Covid Pandemic really brought that home to me. My students mean more to me than they know because of the relationships I have built over the last few years. My journey has brought me to the realization that I am becoming the teacher I was meant to be, even if I had to go through several different hurdles. I am excited for this school year to see my kids and to continue to become a better teacher. My biggest realization is that students' relationships are the reason why we are in the classroom, and if we can have a great relationship with our students, then they will try their hardest.

Becoming the Teacher I was Meant to Be

Jessica Reed, Ed.S.

Jessica Reed is a special education teacher in Georgia, who has been teaching for 11 years. Jessica's undergraduate degree is in Elementary Education from the University of Kentucky. She has a Masters of Arts in Collaborative Teaching (6-12) from the University of Alabama. She received her ED.S. in Instructional Technology from Kennesaw State University. Jessica is a certified Google for Education Trainer and a Google Innovator (#NYC19).

Jessica is married to Robby and they have one daughter, Elizabeth (3). Jessica is an avid UKY alumni who loves to present at conferences and make connections with teachers from all over the world to discuss how collaboration can be effective in the classroom.

25

OVERCOMING BARRIERS & FINDING MY PASSION

REGINA A. MOORE, M.ED

Passion

What is passion? What does it mean to you? What it means to me - finding what I love, immersing myself in it, and then continuing to expand on that love. Several years ago, I found one of my passions in technology. However, finding my way to fulfill that passion had been a challenge. Finding my passion in a job in technology continues to be a challenge. My dream is to become a Technology Trainer in Educational Technology or an Educational Instructional Designer. I continue to share my passion with other educators while searching and applying for the job of my dreams and patiently waiting for it to come my way.

My Journey

This journey began over five years ago when I made an appointment with the Graduate Career Counselor at Loyola University. As an alumnus, this was a service offered by the university. She gave me a career assessment to complete and a week later we reviewed the results. Technology was off the charts. She even commented that she had never seen results that high in one area. I discussed with her that I enjoyed working in education but would like to find a job that incorporated my love and passion for technology. She did not have any suggestions for me and never mentioned the Educational Technology (ET) Degree Program that Loyola offered. We discussed that I should continue taking technology classes at the local community college as I had been doing all along. It was a year later, merely by accident, when I was in my SPAM email at work and discovered an email about all the master's degree programs that Loyola University offered. One, in particular, caught my eye: the ET Program. My prayers had been answered. One barrier had been overcome.

The next barrier to overcome would be getting accepted into the program. The university had cohorts available for educators. I called and spoke with an admissions representative to obtain more information about how the cohort worked. I asked about joining a different county cohort that was offered closer to where I lived versus joining the county cohort where I worked. That was not a problem. The degree was a two-year program, 36 credits consisting of six credits per semester, 8 weeks per class. The classes would take place at Loyola's Howard County location every Tuesday. This would be a commitment, but I was definitely up to the task. I applied and was accepted. In August of 2016, my ET journey began.

Little did I know that some of my coworkers would be another barrier of mine; another challenge for me to rise above, their hesitation of becoming 21st century educators. I offered my technology expertise to try and make our job easier and was often met with resistance. Personally, I think some just felt I might be trying to take away their control rather than make their work easier tasks to complete. This did not discourage me; I kept offering my suggestions and continue to do so to this day. A coworker of mine tells me all the time,

I light up like Christmas when I talk about technology and share with her new skills I have learned. She wants to learn. She is fascinated by the female tech brain, and this inspires me to continue to share my knowledge with her and others. She and some of the other school counselors allowed me to try out my new skills and brainstormed with me when I had class projects to complete. With a recent change in staff, I have found less resistance, and they embrace my knowledge. I am all about the motto work smarter, not harder.

Sharing Knowledge

The ET Program was a fantastic experience. I had already found my passion, but because of this program I am able to utilize it, continue to expand that knowledge, push myself beyond my limits, make connections with educators that never would have been possible all the while doing what I love. It has made it all worth it. Prior to graduating in September 2018, I became a Google Certified Educator Level 1 and a Microsoft Office Specialist in PowerPoint and Excel. I had become an expert in Google Sites and completely revamped my department's website. I also decided it was time to streamline the registration process for the upcoming school year. We needed a better way to share information with students and families, and track students' course selections once they completed their registration. I created another Google Site and posted all this information. Students would no longer complete their registration on paper; they would fill out a Google Form. After the first spring that the new registration process was completed, I asked the counselors for feedback. My revamping was met with success, and no one had suggestions for any changes. I again asked for feedback at the beginning of the second year and still was told it was fine, it worked well, there was no need for changes.

The year 2020 has been met with many barriers for educators across the country. In March, school was shut down, and a world of virtually educating children began. Educators had to figure out in a matter of days how to teach students from home while navigating their own life during a pandemic. As school counselors, we had to certify graduates and finalize the school year from home. Once the school year ended, educators waited impatiently all summer, and again, we were to begin another school year virtually. I continue to search for a technology training position. All I kept thinking and hoping is due to the pandemic there has to be a greater need for educational trainers. I continue to apply and wait. I email contacts and patiently wait. I interview and patiently wait. While I am thankful to have a job, I wait to overcome this barrier. In the meantime, I am asked to offer Professional Development to the staff at school, and was asked to assist the Technology Training Team (T3) with a Virtual Google Certified Educator Level 1 Bootcamp and participated in the Google Certified Educator Level 2 Bootcamp. Passing the Level 2 exam was a wonderful feeling. It enhanced that already excited feeling I get when I talk about technology.

My advice to those who come up against barriers, never give up, never stop dreaming, never stop pushing because eventually dreams do come true. With each barrier I face I do my best to rise to the challenge. One day at a time and one goal at a time make each dream a reality.

Overcoming Barriers & Finding My Passion

Regina A. Moore

Regina A. Moore is a School Counselor at Bowie High School, located in Prince George's County, MD. She has been working in education since 1997. Regina is a Microsoft Office Specialist in Excel and PowerPoint, 2013. She is also a Google Certified Educator Level 1, and recently earned her Google Certified Educator Level 2. She has a Bachelor of Arts degree from Salisbury University, a Master of Education degree in School Counseling from Loyola University, an Administration 1 Certification from McDaniel College, and most recently, she graduated from Loyola University in September 2018 with a Master of Education degree in Educational Technology. Regina would like to change careers and work as an Instructional Designer or an Educational Technology Trainer, specifically training teachers and staff helping them continue their growth as 21st century educators.

26

YOU AND OTHER YS

LYNN THOMAS

The important factor is YOU.

You

John Hattie, in his ground-breaking work Visible Learning, concluded that teachers are among the most powerful influences in learning. He found that a "teacher's beliefs and commitments are the greatest influence on student achievement" (Hattie, 2012, p. 25). Teachers do this by constantly evaluating and assessing, not just students, but their teaching methods and the effectiveness of those methods and strategies. A*re students engaged? Are they showing deep understanding? Are they making connections?* are questions we pose to ourselves every day. We look at cognitive engagement, focus on problem-solving and teaching strategies that relate to the content, work to impart new knowledge and monitor for fluency and understanding, provide feedback, have a deep understanding of how we learn, and work to see learning through the students' eyes to adjust appropriately. Hattie goes on to say that this focus "needs to be shared by all in a school" and that "there is a strong link between sustained focus across all involved within a school and improved student achievement" (Hattie, 2012, p. 23). This shared focus is often called collective efficacy. Combined, collective efficacy and individual teacher efficacy are among the greatest factors in influencing student success. In other words, YOU, fellow teacher -- as part of a team and as an individual -- are important and vital.

Yikes

This year has turned everything on its head – including many teachers' confidence levels. Pivoting to remote learning, using new digital tools, rethinking the way we teach everything, was a stressful experience for everyone – downright harrowing for many! Knowing that trying new challenges at the best of times can shake our confidence level, it is only too easy to see how confidence levels were rocked during remote emergency learning during a global pandemic. Working as a collective supporting each other has never been so important. I know I depended on my network of teacher friends to commiserate with, bounce ideas off of, share struggles and collaborate with to solve those problems. Confidence might be personal, but it is strongly affected by the support and feedback we gain through and with our collective networks.

Yo-Yo

Add to the shaken confidence syndrome daily drastic changes and feeling like a yo-yo becomes the understatement of the year. For example, just when many teachers got a handle on new learning platforms, reformatting lessons, check-ins and phone calls, new parameters were thrust upon us – you MUST teach synchronously! And this demand amidst alarming reservations about online safety, privacy, and equity issues. Even though we share resources and strategies and support each other in times of need, this was a further hit to the confidence of teachers and their professional judgment.

Yearning for Yesterday

I don't know about you, but John Lennon's song was on a constant loop in my head…even though I logically know that yearning for yesterday is completely unproductive and perhaps even detrimental to my own mental well-being. A natural part of the grieving process for everything we knew that was lost, at least for a time, or who knows how long? We can all understand the process, and we all crawled through it in one way or another these past few months. This grief process was communally shared, but it is still yet another hit for the psyche.

Yardstick

Part of the problem is the yardstick we measure ourselves against. I'm really not sure if it's a yard, a mile, a minute, or a millennium that we are supposed to be measuring at this point, but whatever it is, it seems to keep moving and changing. First of all, we can't use the yardstick we always have – we are not teaching in the times we always have. Even if we go back to classrooms like we always have, it will be vastly different and not just because of adding safety measures, PPE, social distancing, etc. We have to take into account how everything, including us, has changed. DRASTICALLY. Similar to understanding that we can't mimic the classroom perfectly in online teaching because it doesn't translate, we can no longer use or strive for the same measures we did before – they don't translate.

Let's look at some numbers outlined by Marc Brackett in his book Permission to Feel (italics are my added commentary):

- "According to a 2014 Gallop poll, 46% of teachers felt high levels of daily stress throughout the school year" (Brackett, 2019). Imagine what that number is now, during COVID, with many districts' back-to-school plans underwhelming and insufficient to alleviate stress levels of teachers, students or parents.
- "According to the 2019 World Happiness Report, negative feelings, including worry, sadness, and anger, have been rising around the world, up by 27% from 2010 to 2018" (Brackett, 2019). The explosion of anger witnessed in the continuing protests and racial unrest coupled with COVID related pressures and worry are all too likely to see this number rise substantially.
- "Anxiety disorders are the most common mental illness in the United States, affecting 25% of children between 13 and 18" (Brackett, 2019). Students have been isolated from their friends and wider family units; some have been enduring unsafe and harmful home situations, food insecurity, and illness; and many are stressed about getting sick or putting someone they love in jeopardy. It is difficult to think that these numbers HAVEN'T grown significantly.

Faced with these statistics, our whole approach needs to focus on well-being, emotional intelligence and social-emotional learning. Students may not only have learning gaps from school closures and remote learning, they may need significant support before they are even able to start focusing on curriculum content.

You

That brings us back to YOU. In all this, the important factor is YOU. Your well-being translates into a confident, caring adult who sees past the worry and anxiety, the trauma, the possible behaviours, to the child and that child's potential. You are a really big deal in the future success of students. No matter what crazy scheme, pivot, or expectation is put in place, you're the most powerful influence on a child's success. SO, don't worry about some silly unrealistic yardstick – remember those yardsticks are so yesterday! And we all know yearning for yesterday is unproductive. Focus on today, breathe, and be well. I know I'm trying really hard to do that, and it isn't very easy in this climate, but teachers – we have each other. We are our best support – rely on that.

REFERENCES

>Hattie, J. (2012). Visible learning for teachers maximizing impact on learning. London: Routledge.

>Brackett, M. A. (2019). Permission to feel: Unlocking the power of emotions to help our kids, ourselves, and our society thrive. New York: Celadon Books.

27

TAKE TIME TO REST

MARVIA DAVIDSON

When we choose rest, we improve our wellbeing; it's a way we can love ourselves.

Rest in the Time of a Global Crisis

I remember where I was the day the news came. It was spring break. I was going to spend the whole week doing absolutely nothing related to work. I was going to clean, make art, bake all the delicious things, see family, catch up on reading, engage in all the creative things, and do lots of mental and physical resting. I was going to do so many restful-for-me things, and I needed the break; but then COVID-19 happened, and it shifted everything about this spring break. There was no longer a sense of ease, rest, or creative welcome. Instead, there was a sense of ominous, undefined foreboding as the President of America declared a national emergency due to the Novel Coronavirus. This news was peculiar, frightful, alarming, and unimaginable.

March 2020 is one month I am not likely to forget. It was the month that changed how we did school for the rest of the spring semester as we were suddenly thrust into a 100% remote and crisis schooling situation. Whatever resting I was going to do on spring break quickly vanished. Instead, there was worry, weariness, anxiousness, and a sense of apprehension. It was a challenge to know what to expect. We were susceptible to an invisible threat that could strike at any moment. The sense of the unknown was unsettling. While I wasn't terribly afraid, I also wasn't in a state of peace. My mind spilled over with questions about what was going to happen, how would school resume, and what exactly did "shelter in place" mean? It all sounded scary and foreign to me, and the next few months proved to be some of the most challenging. In many ways, it was challenging for all of us.

We went from working in buildings surrounded by students and colleagues to working from home either alone or surrounded by family. I don't know about others, but the instant shift to virtual, crisis schooling and working, plus the uneasy feelings were surreal. While it was and continues to be a challenging time, one thing I've learned over the last few months is that we must choose rest. It is for our good. When I say rest, I do not only mean sleeping. I discovered there are many ways we can take time to rest in ways that renew our entire being. Resting wasn't just about sleep while Covid19 was splashing all across the news. Resting came to be about the mind, the body, the soul, and learning how to engage in the right-for-me kinds of rest to have the strength, courage, and capacity to walk through the coming months.

Rest Is Learning to Love Ourselves Well

Even before the pandemic began, I wanted to read more of the science of rest. I wanted to practice rest in a way that addressed the whole person. I knew rest was good for the soul and body, and I wanted to know more about the impact rest can have on us. Rather than regale you with all the wonderful books, tools, and resources available, I want to share some things you might consider when it comes to rest. The hope is that you'll engage in a process of rest which invigorates you for life and work.

As educators, we are dedicated to the students we serve and our craft, often at the expense of resting ourselves along the way. We'll do whatever it takes to ensure our students have what they need to succeed in the classroom. We'll stay up hours on end to learn a tool or instructional pedagogy because we're driven to do and be our best. This constant go-go-go is not sustainable. The more the pandemic went on, the more it became clear how we were all being stretched beyond our regular capacity levels, and I am finding that bandwidth (capacity) is precious. It is something we should steward if we want to have healthy longevity in our work and in our lives.

Regardless of a pandemic, the old normal, or what is quickly becoming the ever-shifting, new normal, making a deliberate practice of rest can benefit us for a lifetime. It is imperative we stay tuned in and aware of how we are. Some questions we might ponder to check in with ourselves might be:

- How are we?
- How are we noticing?
- How are we responding physically, spiritually, mentally, emotionally to what we're walking through in this season?
- How are we pushing through?
- How are we ignoring things?
- How are we attending to our souls?
- How are we attending to our bodies?
- How are we taking care of our mental health?
- How are we fostering and nurturing our well-being?

Making rest and physical movement through the Covid19 pandemic caused me to think of these questions more frequently. Finding restful practices became an integral part of dealing with the highs and lows of the collective, extended health crisis our world was facing. Perhaps we can all gently remind ourselves what rest means.

Rest can be a verb, as in ceasing from laboring or engaging in an activity. Rest can be a noun, like a state of being at peace in body, spirit, or mind. There was one definition that stood out to me from Merriam-Webster's online dictionary regarding rest: "something used for support (Rest 2020)." Imagine this idea of rest! How fascinating that rest is something we can do and be!

Rest can support us physically, mentally, spiritually, and emotionally. A consistent message I found as I read and researched rest and being intentional about it is how good it is for the body, mind, and soul. In the following section are five things we might consider to start a practice of resting.

Ways We Can Rest

1. Know your mind. Get alone to know your thoughts and allow your mind to decompress and clear itself. One thing to consider is that mental fatigue can have adverse effects on our bodies, mind, and energy levels (Dalton-Smith, 2017). Be more present to yourself and what you're thinking to cultivate the mental/brain rest you need.
2. Listen to your body. Maybe that means a nap, and that can "improve emotional regulation and self-control" (Pang, 2018, pg. 118). Let the body rest. Maybe it means a workout. Maybe it means a long walk or even lying down to give yourself a bodily reprieve. Maybe it's a day you sabbath or decompress. Perhaps it means we uncomplicate

life by simplifying our personal, top priorities and scheduling rest (Morris, 2019; Pang, 2020). We don't have to obligate ourselves to fill our weekends by doing things that do not help us rest.

3. Reduce digital and sensory overload. Get choosy, particular, and intentional about the digital, social, technology tools you use. We know best how much we're tied to our smart devices or social media tools. Being mindful of how much we take in can help us determine when and how our "clutter is costly" (Newport, 2019, pg. 35). With that digital mindfulness comes a sensory rest where we pay attention to our senses and how they're being overloaded or overstimulated. When we do so, we can address physical and mental stress (Dalton-Smith, 2017). Sometimes we need to unplug from the extra noise, and that can bring about rest too.

4. Pay attention to your emotions. Be aware of how you are responding and dealing with things around you and within you. When we are purposeful in how we choose to rest ourselves, we can "cultivate calm" (Pang, 2018, pg. 243). Since we are more exposed to all the goings-on in the world, our work, and our families through instant digital or technological access, it's important to pay attention to our emotions and how they're impacted by what we're taking in or exposing ourselves to. Doing so can also improve emotional capacity, energy, and connection (Dalton-Smith, 2017). Take care of your emotional needs.

5. Play. Play. Play. In all the seriousness that comes with work and living life, we need a gentle reminder to do things that bring a sense of joy and fun. Engaging in playful forms of rest lets us encounter what it means to have a sense of wonderment (Dalton-Smith, 2017). Make

room for leisure, and perhaps you'll find an "increase in the relaxation you enjoy through your week" (Newport, 2019). Plan, play, and rediscover the beauty of creative, playful rest.

Taking Care of Ourselves

Take care of yourselves, educator friends. This season seems more like a marathon rather than a sprint. Some of us may be experiencing loss. Some of us are aware of how emotionally charged things are around us. Some of us may not know how to handle all the things that are coming at us. Some of us do not know how to ask for the support we need because we're not used to needing to ask for it. Some of us want to be reassured. Some of us are doing better than we expected, while others of us are barely making it. What's important is that you begin to notice and pay attention. Talk about it. Get the help you need.

Find ways of resting that refresh, restore, and renew you. Be choosy and intentional about how you rest too. Here are some questions to consider as you think about your own rest practices:

- Do you need physical, bodily rest? Do that.
- Do you need to give your mind a rest to process through your thoughts and reset your thinking? Do that.
- Do you need to step away from all the social/digital noise? Step away.
- Have you not practiced your creative things in a long time? Take up your practice again.
- Is your spirit languishing or weary? Do your spiritual practices to realign and refresh your soul.
- Missing the sound of peaceful reprieve? Get to your quiet place.

Life is precious. The ability to rest is just as precious and critical. Choose rest. Choose to be still. Choose to take that nap. Choose to take that walk. Choose to do that artistic or creative thing. Choose to do the analog work. Choose to give your eyes time away from the smartphone or television screen. Let yourself rest.

You gotta take care of you. Prioritize rest. You are worth it, always have been and always will be.

Reference List

>Dalton-Smith, S. (2017). Sacred Rest: Recover your life, renew your energy, restore your sanity (1st ed.). New York, NY: FaithWords.

>Morris, R. (2019). Take the Day Off: Receiving God's gift of rest. (1st ed.) New York, NY: FaithWords.

>Newport, C. (2017). Digital minimalism: Choosing a focused life in a noisy world. New York: Portfolio/Penguin.

>Pang, A. S. K. (2018). Rest: Why you get more done when you work less. (1st paperback ed.) New York, NY: Basic Books.

>Rest. (2020). In Merriam-Webster.com. Retrieved October 03, 2020, from https://www.merriam-webster.com/dictionary/rest

MARVIA DAVIDSON

Marvia Davidson

Marvia was a high school English teacher in public, private, and charter schools in Texas before becoming a campus administrator. She is currently serving as a school improvement coordinator. She has worked with students and teachers from diverse backgrounds, and loves helping students realize their potential. As a lifelong learner, Marvia loves growing her PLN, CoffeeEdu meet-ups, and collaborating with educators on how to do what's best for students and teachers to bring positive change. She's not only an educator but an avid mixed media artist who enjoys lettering, painting, and baking. She is committed to learner and teacher development. Connect with Marvia at @marviadavidson on Twitter, Instagram, LinkedIn, and Voxer. You can also find her writing, making, and creating on her site at marviadavidson.com.

ACKNOWLEDGMENTS

We wish to thank our chapter peer editors and thought partners, who helped us to bring the best out of each chapter:

Amanda Zullo
Andrea Cook
Cyndy Harrison
Dan Tricarico
Deborah Kerby
Emmanuel Duncan
Erin Kiger
Jacie Maslyk
Jami Fowler-White
Marvia Davidson
Melissa Dandy Walker
Morgan Venzant
Rachelle Dene Poth
Tisha Poncio
Tracy Kelly

EDUMATCH BOOKS RELEASED IN 2020

January

14: *The Edcorps Classroom* by Chris Aviles

28: *Strive for Happiness in Education* by Rob Dunlop

February

4: *Thinking About Teaching* by Casey Jakubowski

11: *I'm Sorry Story* by Melody McAllister*

17: *Define Your Why* by Barbara Bray

March

20: *Systems, Cycles, Seasons, and Processes* by Emjay Smith

31: *The Tiebreaker* by Rebecca Gibboney*

April

22: *Fur Friends Forever* by LaTezeon Humphrey Balentine

May

10: *The Perfect Puppy* by Kristen Koppers*

15: *Reignite the Flames* by Mandy Froehlich

June

8: *Lessons and Lattes* by Aubrey Jones*

18: *REAL LOVE* by Alexes Terry*

23: *Kwamee & Mattoo: Mystical Adventure to St. Croix* by Laila & SJ Eakins

July

14: *Making Assessment Work for Educators who Hate Data but Love Kids* by David Schmittou

22: *Play? Yay! Baby Talk* by BreAnn Fennell*

28: *Back to Zero* by Dr. Joy

August

11: *Scripted* by Paula Neidlinger, Bruce Reicher*, and Randall Tomes

26: *Agi and the Thought Compass* by Betsy O'Neill-Sheehan

September

1: *Coding to Kindness* by Valerie Sousa

9: *Engagement is Not a Unicorn (It's a Narwhal)* by Heather Lyon

November

1: *The Educator's Matchbook* by Mandy Froehlich

9: *Aubrey Bright in Stories that Connect Us* by Jennifer Casa-Todd and Leigh Cassell

15: *It's Me* by Jeff Kubiak

December

18: *True Story* by Rachelle Dene Poth

31: *EduMatch Snapshot in Education 2020*

Buy in bulk (quantities of 10 or more) and save! Visit edumatchpublishing.com to sign up for our mailing list, and stay in the know about new releases, rewards, contests, and more!

Want to contribute to **EduSnap21**? Visit books.edumatch.org/edusnapinterestform.

*=author appears in *Edusnap20*

www.ingramcontent.com/pod-product-compliance
Lightning Source LLC
Chambersburg PA
CBHW071412070526
44578CB00003B/560